Discussion in the College Classroom

Jay R. Howard

Discussion in the College Classroom

Getting Your Students Engaged and Participating in Person and Online

JB JOSSEY-BASS™
A Wiley Brand

Library of Congress Cataloging-in-Publication Data is on file.

9781118571354 (hbk.)
9781118571798 (ebk.)
9781118571743 (ebk.)

Printed in the United States of America
FIRST EDITION
HB Printing   10 9 8 7 6 5 4 3 2 1

In memory of Eileen T. Bender and Carla B. Howery—two mentors who saw potential in me before I could see it in myself

Contents

Foreword

Classroom interaction—after lecture, it's the most widely used instructional strategy, and it's just about as widely endorsed. How many faculty have you met who don't want students asking, answering, and commenting in class or online? But also like lecture, classroom interaction often fails to reach its potential. In many classrooms, participation must be pulled from reluctant students who would clearly rather not. The verbal few make comments for points, not always because they have points to make. Typically participation is a vertical exchange between the teacher and a student. It takes place in the presence of others but without their involvement. When the teacher attempts a discussion, it's not a lively, engaging exchange of interesting ideas but isolated, superficial observations made by students who don't comment in light of anything in the text or that's been covered in previous class sessions.

"If you could change one thing about participation in your courses, what would you change?" I ask in workshops. Commonly the responses are about more students taking part, and some students taking less part, more real questions and fewer pedantic queries about exam content and paper length, more students being less afraid of wrong answers, and students at least occasionally responding to each other. I don't encounter many faculty who are happy with the extent or kind of interaction that's occurring in their classrooms.

But what's starting to sound like a tale of woe here doesn't have to carry on to an unhappy conclusion. You have in your hands a book full of content with the potential to rewrite the story of student interaction in face-to-face and online courses. Most faculty are not aware that there is an extensive and excellent body of research on students' verbal contributions in courses. It describes how it occurs, why it happens that way, and how some approaches can produce better outcomes than others. This is research with practical implications. It has findings that can be implemented. And the best part of this happier story is that one of the researchers who has done some of the very best work on classroom interaction has authored this book.

I met Jay Howard on a cold day in January. I was working at a campus north of Indianapolis and I mentioned some of his work in one of my sessions. One of his colleagues was there and asked if I'd like to meet him. Indeed! She called and I stopped by his office at Butler University where he is the Dean of Liberal Arts and Sciences. It was only a short meeting but by the time it was over I was all but pleading with him to do a book.

He did and here it is—a detailed map that points the way to better classroom interaction. Along the way you'll learn about phenomena you've observed in your classroom, things like civil attention, the consolidation of responsibility, the role played by norms, and the characteristics of those students who talk a lot and others who won't talk at all. Jay is a sociologist and that discipline frames how he has studied and understands classroom interaction. It's a useful frame with much theory and research supporting these more specific conclusions about classroom interaction.

What I especially love about this book is that even though it's written by a researcher, it doesn't read like any research article you've ever read. The various chapters start with descriptions of classroom interaction experiences we've all had and the feelings they engender—the frustration of trying to get students engaged, the anger at how passive their approach is to everything, and the disappointed tiredness that makes more effort seem futile. And from these familiar places, Jay leads us to relevant research. It explains these student responses and explores alternatives. Suggestions offered in the book come from the research and from practice—what teachers have learned as they've tried to cultivate the kind of interaction that promotes learning. Jay draws from his teaching experience and references that of other teachers as well.

The book also highlights the research of others, not just Jay's work. In fact I kept pushing him to acknowledge his work, to own it in his writing. Many of his studies involved students as co-researchers. They are listed as authors, which makes his work all the more laudable to my way of thinking. The book's coverage of the research and literature on classroom interaction is extensive. No other resource looks as broadly across disciplines or offers as integrative an analysis of student interaction as you'll find in this book.

There is a real need for new forms of pedagogical scholarship. A traditional review of research pieces on classroom interaction is fine for those interested in the next studies needed in this area. It is not what those of us trying to promote dialogue in our courses need. Certainly our practice will benefit from a good working knowledge of the research. It explains much of what we see and find frustrating. At an emotional level, it's comforting. The lack of response, the passivity, the failure to engage and connect isn't just happening in our courses. It's not because the way we're handling interaction is particularly inept. But we need more than a working knowledge of this research—we need help with implications. How do we revise policies and practices in light of it? Here's a book that responds to both needs. It establishes a knowledge base and guides decision making based on what has been discovered.

That's not to imply that all the research on classroom interaction is conclusive, that all the findings are consistent, or that all the implications prescribe clear-cut actions. This is social science research, after all, and classroom interaction is a complex phenomenon. How interaction is handled in a large class isn't the same as how it's handled in a small class. How questions are framed in a science class isn't how they are formed in a literature class. How one teacher executes a Socratic questioning sequence isn't how another teacher does it. So, not all the answers are easy, obvious, or the same. But the answers and advice given in this book offer places to begin. They provide the foundation for the policies and practices we can use to promote participation and discussion.

It is time for us to move beyond experientially derived how-to-teach books. They were fine when what we had was mostly the wisdom of practice. Our pedagogical knowledge now rests on a firmer foundation. We do learn from experience, but we can learn more from systematic inquiry and analysis, especially when it comes from someone who's done the research, been in the classroom, and writes with the caring commitment of a trusted colleague. Welcome to Jay Howard's *Discussion in the College Classroom: Getting Your Students Engaged and Participating in Person and Online.*

Maryellen Weimer
September 2014

Acknowledgments

As a sociologist, it should come as no surprise that I recognize the importance of context and community. I have been fortunate throughout my career to be a member of communities that have prioritized teaching and learning. This was true in my undergraduate days at Indiana University South Bend where the faculty took an interest in me as a first-generation, nontraditional student and in my graduate school days at the University of Notre Dame where my efforts in teaching as well as scholarship were affirmed and encouraged.

I have been a part of both Indiana and Butler universities—two institutions that value teaching and learning. At IU, I became part of a group, the Faculty Colloquium on Excellence in Teaching, which brought together award-winning teachers from all eight campuses. As the old marketing pitch went, IU was "one university with eight front doors." However, at Indiana University–Purdue University Columbus, where I spent most of my time, we were not an independent campus but rather a center of Indiana University–Purdue University Indianapolis; we didn't qualify as a front door. So we referred to ourselves as IU's "basement window." But even from the basement window I was welcomed into the community and nurtured as teacher-scholar.

I have also been privileged to be a part of two professional associations, the North Central Sociological Association (NCSA) and the American Sociological Association (ASA), which have long and proud histories of focusing attention on teaching and learning. I was silly enough to volunteer to chair the NCSA Teaching Committee as a second-year assistant professor and a year or two later volunteered to run for the American Sociological Association's Section on Undergraduate Education's Council. To my surprise, I found myself in both roles. (A little hint for graduate students and junior faculty: these are voluntary organizations. They need free labor.) I wish to express my heartfelt thanks to all the members of these communities who shaped me and nurtured me along the way.

I also wish to thank my family for their love and support: my wife, Brenda, and my children, Amalia and Dylan. I also want to thank Priscilla Cobb and Cynthia Drouin, who faithfully guarded my office door and kept my calendar clear of meetings to ensure that the time I blocked out for writing was not intruded upon. Finally, I wish to thank the many students in my research methods courses over the years who conducted studies with me, especially those who became co-authors of the resulting publications that significantly shaped the content of this book: Lillard Short, Susan Clark, Amanda Henney, Roberta Baird, George "Chip" James, David Taylor, Aimee Zoeller, and Yale Pratt.

It takes a community, or perhaps I should say it takes communities, to raise a teacher. I am grateful for the influence of these communities in my life.

Preface

In one sense this book began in a sociological social psychology course I took as an undergraduate. One selection in the edited volume required for the course was an excerpt from Karp and Yoels' (1976) groundbreaking sociological examination of the college classroom. I was quite struck by the study and wondered how the results would be different if conducted at a campus like my own—a commuter campus with many nontraditional students. A number of years later, as a new assistant professor, I engaged students in my research methods course to find out. Over the years, numerous classes of students have worked with me to explore the nature of interaction in the college classroom. Some of them have been co-authors of the resulting publications. We were doing research in the scholarship of teaching and learning before we knew it was called the scholarship of teaching and learning.

In another sense this book began with a surprise visit by Maryellen Weimer to my office during the semester break in early January 2012. Dr. Weimer had been at a nearby campus leading a faculty development workshop. When she cited my work in her presentation, a number of people in attendance informed her that I was less than an hour away and would be an easy stop on her drive back to the airport. Simultaneously, I started receiving emails and text messages from colleagues at the workshop asking if I was available to chat with Maryellen. I was. During our conversation, Maryellen suggested I should consider writing a book about discussion as a classroom pedagogy for Jossey-Bass. As a dean, I wasn't sure I could make the time to write a book. But one thing led to another and this book is the outcome of that conversation.

Maryellen was quite persuasive in suggesting that there was a need for a book on the uses of discussion as a classroom pedagogy that was thoroughly informed by the scholarship on the topic. That is precisely what I have sought to provide. I utilize research on student participation in discussion in the college classroom, frame it sociologically, and offer advice and guidance on how we can more effectively facilitate student learning through engagement in discussion. Each chapter begins with a vignette with which I hope you will be able to identify. The vignettes lay out common challenges in utilizing discussion. The chapter that then follows examines the research related to these challenges and offers advice for successfully implementing discussion.

The book begins by identifying and explaining some key college classroom norms (civil attention and the consolidation of responsibility) and points out how these norms can easily undermine the effectiveness of discussion. However, because norms are social constructions, they can be changed. You don't have to allow these to be the operative norms in your courses. From there we move to an examination of how students see and define the college classroom and their own, as well as the instructor's, role in it. When students and faculty define the classroom differently it can undermine the effectiveness of discussion as a tool to facilitate learning. I then consider discussion online by summarizing the research on the topic and utilizing it to offer advice that can help lead to productive and beneficial discussion in an online format. Finally, I address a number of common concerns, or conundrums, related to the use of discussion as a classroom pedagogy. These include whether and how to grade student participation in discussion, how to help students recognize the learning that is happening in discussions that can be messy and circuitous, and how to balance a desire to ensure that necessary content is covered in the course with the use of class discussion.

This book is written, first and foremost, for faculty members who wish to find ways to more effectively facilitate student learning. It is intended to be helpful to both new instructors and experienced ones who are seeking to refresh their pedagogical toolbox. While it is thoroughly grounded in the scholarship of teaching and learning research, it is also intended to be very readable and very practical. The goal is to assist college and university instructors as they seek to become more effective. This book will also be helpful to investigators conducting research on student participation in college classroom discussion. In each chapter, I summarize the research literature related to the topic.

I have benefited throughout my career from the advice, experiences, and expertise of many colleagues who are dedicated to ensuring and maximizing student learning. I hope to pay it forward through this book by being helpful to others who are journeying on that same path with me.

About the Author

J ay R. Howard is Professor of Sociology and Dean of the College of Liberal Arts and Sciences at Butler University in Indianapolis. Previously, he served as Interim Vice Chancellor and Dean, Assistant Dean for Budget and Planning, Head of the Division of Liberal Arts, and Professor of Sociology at Indiana University–Purdue University Columbus (IUPUC).

He is author of over 50 publications on topics ranging from the scholarship of teaching and learning to religion and popular culture. His previous book, co-authored with Nancy A. Greenwood, Indiana University Kokomo, is *First Contact: Teaching and Learning in Introductory Sociology* (Rowman & Littlefield, 2011). He is editor of *Discussion in the College Classroom: Applications for Sociology Instruction* (American Sociological Association, 2004). His book, co-authored with John M. Streck, *Apostles of Rock: The Splintered World of Contemporary Christian Music* (University Press of Kentucky, 1999) was named a 2000 Choice Magazine Outstanding Academic Title.

Dr. Howard has served as Deputy Editor of the American Sociological Association journal, *Teaching Sociology*. He is a Fellow of the P. A. Mack Center at Indiana University for Inquiry on Teaching and Learning and has served as president of the North Central Sociological Association. He is the recipient of numerous awards, including the 2013 ASA Distinguished Contributions to Teaching Award, the 2009 P. A. Mack Award for Distinguished Service to Teaching from Indiana University, the 2008 Hans O. Mauksch Award for Distinguished Contributions to Undergraduate Education from the ASA Section on Teaching and Learning, and the 2001 NCSA Distinguished Contributions to Teaching Award. He earned a BA in Sociology from Indiana University South Bend, and an MA and PhD in Sociology from University of Notre Dame.

1

Introduction: Why Bother with Classroom Discussion?

The class session has been moving along nicely as you cover important material in your lecture when your students' body language tells you that you are losing them. Some are propping up their heads with arms and hands. Others have stopped making eye contact as they gaze off to the side. Faces glaze over while students shuffle distractedly in their seats. It appears a few are texting—only semi-covertly. Others appear to be surfing the web on their laptops—probably checking Facebook again. Yours has been the only voice heard in the classroom for at least 30 minutes now. So, on impulse, you decide to switch gears. Instead of pointing out the pros and cons of the competing perspectives you have just summarized for the class, in hopes of waking them up and getting their brains back into gear, you ask students to compare and contrast the perspectives.

But your worst fears materialize. You are greeted by blank stares, if the students look at you at all. You pause, hoping at least one student will speak up and venture to offer a comment. You rephrase the question to give students a little more time to consider their views on the matter. You notice the hum of the fluorescent lights as you begin to feel the uncomfortable silence. It's clear now that most are trying to avoid eye contact with you lest they be called upon. Some are thumbing through the textbook looking for clues as to how they should respond. Internally, you are shaking your head. Isn't it obvious that the question calls for students to compare and contrast, to weigh the merits of the two perspectives, identify strengths and weaknesses, and bring their own values and judgments to bear on them? There is no single "correct answer" to be found in the pages of the text. After a seeming eternity, you give up and begin to offer your own assessment of the strengths and weaknesses of the competing perspectives, hoping that at the least you are modeling the process of comparing and contrasting.

After class, you find yourself asking, why is this discussion stuff so difficult? With all the talk at faculty development workshops about the need to engage students in the classroom and how students supposedly both enjoy such pedagogies and learn more effectively when they are utilized, why doesn't it seem to work for you when theory meets the hard realities of classroom practice? Why not simply stick to the lecture? You can cover more material that way. Why struggle to get students talking when you're not convinced they will have anything worthwhile to say? Is the effort required to engage students worth it?

Yet, there are other times when students take you by surprise. A thoughtful discussion erupts in class seemingly spontaneously. Students get excited about a topic and engage with energy and enthusiasm. They may not always be the most well-informed on the topic, but at least they are showing interest. Of course, some students speak up more than others. In fact, it would be nice if a couple of them spoke less frequently, and what about Tameka sitting in the second row toward the side? She turned in what was easily the best paper in the class on that last assignment. Why won't she share her insights? Still there are enough students participating to have a thoughtful, well-rounded conversation on the topic. Sometimes students take the class on tangents that are particularly insightful. Where did that come from? It's clear that a number have actually read the assignment by their references to the book. This is what makes college teaching so rewarding! It's one of those moments when students "own" their education and seize opportunities to learn—not just from you, the faculty member, but from each other. You leave class energized, affirmed, and renewed in your commitment to facilitate student learning and to develop their critical thinking skills.

On the walk back to your office, you ponder, what can I do to ensure exciting, helpful conversations like these happen more frequently? They seem to be spontaneous, not easily created. Sure, sometimes you succeed in igniting such beneficial discussions, but you're not getting any younger. It's getting increasingly hard to predict what topics or what aspects of a topic will grab the attention of students and spark that exciting moment of learning in your classes.

If you have found yourself in similar situations, both times when discussions fall flat and times when they succeed in unexpected ways, you are not alone. The majority of college and university faculty members take teaching and learning seriously. We want to do well by our students. We want them to learn and we want to help. We find intrinsic value and excitement in our discipline's content and we want our students to share in that excitement. Igniting the spark that creates the blaze of engaged learning and critical thinking is one of the great rewards of being a college professor. Yet it sometimes seems like a one-way street—we do all the work in the attempt to make learning happen as our students sit by passively waiting to be spoon-fed.

Facilitating an effective discussion in class feels like hard work sometimes. Is it worth it? Are the benefits sufficient to justify the effort? How can discussions be managed in such a way as to increase the likelihood of success and avoid those painfully awkward silences or one-word answers that do nothing more than barely scratch the surface?

Yes, effective discussions are hard work—all good teaching requires significant effort. Great teachers are made, not born. In this book I will argue that while facilitating effective discussions takes forethought, planning, and structure, it is well worth the effort and makes the experience of teaching much more enjoyable. However, too often faculty members assume that worthwhile discussions merely happen spontaneously in class. And sometimes they do. But just as an effective lecture takes preparation, planning, and structure in order to facilitate student learning, so does an effective discussion. An effective discussion in the college classroom is much less frequently the result of a lucky happenstance. It is more likely to be the result of forethought and intentional planning.

Benefits of Engaging Students in Discussion

The first and most important reason to tackle the hard work of facilitating an effective discussion is that students learn more as a result. This is a rather bold claim that will be supported as the book unfolds, but I want to point out here that discussion is one way in which faculty members can actively engage students in the classroom. And over the past 30 years with the expansion of scholarship of teaching and learning research in higher education, there is an abundance of evidence that points to the value of active learning and student engagement in facilitating learning (see, for example, Pascarella and Terenzini 1991, 2005).

Chickering and Gamson's (1987) summary of the research on effective classroom practices is one of the first and most influential efforts to draw attention to the value of active learning—one of their seven principles for good practice in undergraduate education. Since that time scholars in many disciplines have been investigating and articulating the benefits of active learning. Kuh et al. (2005) conclude that student engagement is a key to academic success. They note that students learn more when they are intensely involved in their own education and have the opportunity to think about and apply what they are learning.

Prince (2004) in his review of the research concludes there is broad support for all forms of active learning. As an engineering educator, Prince (2004) notes that despite a tendency in his field to "push through as much material as possible" (p. 229), students will learn more if lectures are interrupted with brief activities that engage students. In their review of the research, Bonwell and Eison (1991) conclude that active learning strategies are comparable to lecture in terms of promoting mastery of content, but are superior to lecture in promoting the development of thinking and writing skills. To be engaged in active learning, students must do more than passively listen in class. They need to read, write, discuss, and solve problems while engaging in higher-order thinking skills such as evaluation, synthesis, and analysis (Bonwell and Eison 1991).

Discussion versus Participation

While active learning can take many forms, our primary focus here is on students' verbal participation in class discussions. While some faculty define participation as including things such as attending class or actively listening, when students verbally participate they maximize their engagement and their learning. Students can and do learn simply by attending class and absorbing what they can, by being prepared for class—having completed homework and reading assignments, and by being active listeners—carefully adhering to the presentation of ideas and insights by their professor and their classmates (Howard 2005). While Reda (2009) argues that some students value speaking and silence differently than does the contemporary culture of American higher education, when students verbally interact with the material, the professor, and their classmates they are most actively engaged and most likely to be learning and developing thinking skills. Nonetheless, as Reda (2009) cautions, speaking does not automatically result in learning. And some students may perceive demands to speak out in the classroom as a high-stakes, anxiety-inducing form of verbal testing. Therefore, it is important to remember that discussion occurs in many forms.

Participation in discussion can take the form of occasional questions or comments in the class as a whole, interacting with others in a small group or even pairs, or making more formal oral presentations to the class. Whereas large-group discussion might be perceived as quite threatening, participation in smaller groups or pairs may be perceived as safe by our more introverted students. The benefits of this participation in class discussion, whether in large or small groups, are well documented.

When students are actively participating in discussion they learn more than when they merely listen (Kuh et al. 2005). In two national surveys, Umbach and Wawrzynski (2005) found that students reported greater learning when faculty utilized active and collaborative learning pedagogies. On a smaller scale, Murray and Lang (1997) in their study of students in a psychology course found that students who participated more frequently in class discussion earned higher exam grades and students generally learned more when topics were taught using active participation compared to topics taught strictly by lecture. Kuh et al. (2005) stress the importance of students interacting with faculty, both inside and outside class, for development of thinking skills necessary for solving practical problems. In an intriguing study that utilized an experimental design in two zoology courses with pre- and post-test assessments, Bodensteiner (2012) found that students in the course that utilized discussion learned and retained information better, as well as felt more confidence in their answers, than students who received content-only instruction. Numerous additional studies have found that active participation in classroom discussion leads to greater student learning (Astin 1985; Johnson, Johnson, and Smith 1991; Kember and Gow 1994, McKeachie 1990).

In addition to increased learning, participation in class discussion also leads to the development of thinking skills. Smith (1977) found that student participation, encouragement, and peer-to-peer interaction was consistently and positively related to the development of critical thinking skills. Crone (1997), Garside (1996), and Greenlaw and DeLoach (2003) each found that active participation in discussion led to improvements in students' critical thinking.

Other benefits to students resulting from participation in class discussion include greater motivation (Junn 1994), improved communication skills (Berdine 1986; Dancer and Kamvounias 2005), and, not surprisingly, higher grades (Handelsman et al. 2005). In many cases, utilizing classroom discussion versus lecture alone makes class more interesting and enjoyable for both students and faculty. It also makes students co-creators in their own learning and promotes a more democratic classroom (Brookfield and Preskill 2005).

Brookfield and Preskill (2005, 21–22) summarize the many benefits of effective classroom discussion for student learning in 15 arguments.

1. It helps students explore a diversity of perspectives.
2. It increases students' awareness of and tolerance for ambiguity or complexity.
3. It helps students recognize and investigate their assumptions.
4. It encourages attentive, respectful listening.
5. It develops new appreciation for continuing differences.
6. It increases intellectual agility.
7. It helps students become connected to a topic.
8. It shows respect for students' voices and experiences.
9. It helps students learn the processes and habits of democratic discourse.
10. It affirms students as co-creators of knowledge.
11. It develops the capacity for the clear communication of ideas and meaning.
12. It develops habits of collaborative learning.
13. It increases breadth and makes students more empathetic.
14. It helps students develop skills of synthesis and integration.
15. It leads to transformation.

At a time when, judging by talking heads on cable TV and by partisan bloggers, many Americans seem to have lost the ability to engage in reasoned, respectful debate and dialogue, encouraging the development of skills and dispositions necessary for civil discourse is particularly important. College classrooms can and should be a place where the skills necessary to be an effective citizen are developed and practiced. Yet, as Brookfield and Preskill (2005) acknowledge, these benefits are not accrued automatically.

Challenges in Utilizing Classroom Discussion

Effective discussion that generates these rewards requires a set of classroom norms to facilitate them. When sociologists discuss the idea of norms, they are referring to unwritten "rules" that guide our behavior in social situations, that is, when we are interacting with other people. Typically, norms are taken for granted to such an extent that typically we notice them only when they are being violated. The vast majority of the time we adhere to norms without giving them much thought. We merely take them for granted as how things are or how one *ought* to behave. For example, when you got up this morning you got dressed without consciously thinking that in our society we have a norm that says people should wear clothing in public. Even more, you probably chose clothing appropriate for the particular settings you would be entering. If you were headed to a basketball game, you most likely chose to wear clothing that was quite different from what you would wear if you were heading to work in your office on campus or to attend a wedding.

All sorts of social situations have norms associated with them. Take, for example, the simple act of riding on an elevator. There is a long list of elevator norms that you very likely follow without giving the matter much thought. What is the first thing you do when you get on an elevator? No, the answer is not "push the button for the desired floor." Before you can do that, you must turn around and face the elevator door. Imagine you are waiting for the elevator.

The doors open and there in the middle of the elevator I stand facing the rear of the elevator. Would you get on the elevator or wait for the next one to come along? Odds are good that, at the very least, you would be quite uncomfortable riding in the elevator with me if I were facing the "wrong" way. Is there a law that says elevator occupants must face the front of the elevator? Of course not, but we all follow the norm that says we should face the front when riding on an elevator.

There are also personal-space norms for elevators. Where do you stand when you are the only person on the elevator? You stand wherever you wish. But as soon as a second person gets on, an invisible line is magically drawn down the center of the elevator. You each stay on your own side of that line. When a third and fourth person boards the elevator, we further subdivide the personal space. Imagine if I boarded the elevator with you and instead of staying on my side, I chose to stand beside you, nearly making physical contact. You would likely shuffle a bit away from me. You definitely would feel uneasy. You may even choose to shove me away or tell me to "back off!" There is no rule posted in the elevator that says I cannot stand close to you on an elevator, but to do so violates a social norm.

Norms in the College Classroom

Just as elevators are a social setting with many taken-for-granted norms that guide our behavior, college classrooms are also chock-full of norms that guide faculty and student behaviors. Take, for example, student seating. On the first day of class, have you ever arrived in your assigned room to find a student seated at the professor's desk or standing behind the podium ready to lead the class session? Never? Why not? That seat might even be more comfortable than the tablet armchair students typically have available to them. While the professor's chair may be more desirable, it is highly unlikely that any student would sit behind the professor's desk or stand at the podium because our social norms indicate that space is reserved for the professor. Throughout their high school experience students likely had assigned seats in each of their classes where they were required to sit every day as the practice facilitated the taking of attendance or perhaps helped avoid behavioral problems that might result from close friends sitting near each other. Students probably complained about this practice and a quick Google search will reveal students complaining about this practice in online forums. In contrast, typically, there are no assigned seats in college classrooms. Students are free to change seats whenever they wish. But what usually happens? Students spend the rest of the semester sitting in the exact same chairs they selected on the first day of class—even if they would prefer a different spot. Should one student switch seats after a few class sessions, another student is likely to feel that "his" or "her" seat has been unfairly taken away by a classmate. While the offended student is unlikely to make too much of a fuss, he or she will feel at least momentarily uncomfortable and perhaps annoyed with the norm-violating classmate.

There are also norms that have quite a bit to do with the interaction that does or does not occur in the typical college classroom. These are norms that are rarely articulated and are merely taken for granted, yet they have significant impact on student learning.

Sociologists David Karp and William Yoels (1976) were among the first to investigate discussion norms in the college classroom. In particular, Karp and Yoels (1976) found that while faculty members tend to define the college classroom as a *focused* environment, students define it as an *unfocused* environment (p. 435). In a focused environment, participants are expected to interact with one another. In an unfocused environment, while interaction is possible, participants do not feel obligated to interact. In a more recent study, Roberts (2002) found that while 82 percent of the faculty in his sample saw the classroom as a focused environment, only 55 percent of his student sample shared that understanding (p. 12). This can lead to some tensions between faculty and students as we define the classroom and its normative expectations differently. If faculty members prod or pressure students to verbally participate when students do not see it as their responsibility, students may take offense. The faculty member may even pay a price for this disconnect in understanding of classroom expectations in the end-of-semester evaluations as students may accuse the professor of making unfair demands of them or being unfriendly toward them.

Students and, very often, faculty are complicit in creating and reinforcing classroom norms that allow the majority of students to avoid participation in classroom discussion. Karp and Yoels (1976) identified particular norms that reinforce this situation. One norm they termed *civil attention*. In most college classrooms, unlike elementary and secondary school classrooms, students do not have to pay attention. Instead, the real expectation is that students pay civil attention.

What's the difference between actually paying attention and paying only civil attention? In college classrooms, civil attention requires that students create the appearance of paying attention. How do they do that? They do so in a large number of ways: occasional nodding of the head; chuckling at appropriate times when the professor attempts to be humorous; making occasional but fleeting eye contact with the faculty member (prolonged eye contact invites verbal interaction); taking notes (or at least appearing to be taking notes); and, merely keeping eyes open and facing the front. Of course, we all have occasional students who violate this norm by closing their eyes, putting their heads down on their desk, reading a newspaper, surfing the web, texting, or engaging in whispered side conversations with classmates. However, many if not most faculty members find this behavior both distracting and offensive. It violates our taken-for-granted norms for classroom behavior. Frequently you can find statements on course syllabi specifically prohibiting many of these behaviors as faculty members attempt to make clear that at a minimum civil attention is the norm in our classrooms.

Igniting the Spark of Engaged Learning through Discussion: What Lies Ahead

In this book I invite you to join in igniting the spark of learning by engaging students in participation in classroom discussion. I present research-based findings regarding classroom norms and how they impact discussion. We will find that students are not equally likely to participate: Which students are most likely to participate and why do they choose to do so? Which students typically choose not to participate in discussion and why do they choose not to do so? Utilizing research results, I offer a variety of strategies for engaging more students with the goal of increasing student learning. Perhaps some of these strategies will be familiar to you already, but knowing the research foundations for their use will hopefully increase both your commitment to use them and your confidence in doing so. Other strategies may be completely new to you and may spark some creative thinking about how to adapt and implement them in your courses.

Chapter 2 provides an in-depth exploration of the norm of civil attention and explains why students can get by without actually paying attention in the college classroom. I also identify the ways in which faculty members are complicit in the development and reinforcement of this classroom norm. But I won't leave you hanging. Chapter 2 addresses strategies for overcoming the norm of civil attention and engaging students in classroom discussion.

In Chapter 3, I address another classroom discussion norm identified by Karp and Yoels (1976): the consolidation of responsibility. The norm of the consolidation of responsibility means that in any college classroom, regardless of size, a very small number of students (three to seven) will account for 75–95 percent of student verbal contributions. We use the extensive scholarship on this topic to show which students are most likely to accept the consolidation of responsibility and become the dominant talkers and which are more likely to choose to remain silent or participate only rarely.

We explore research-based evidence regarding why students choose to participate in discussion and why they often choose not to participate. Chapter 3 concludes with strategies for overcoming the consolidation of responsibility and increasing student participation in discussion.

In Chapter 4 I explore the differing definitions faculty and students, as well as different groups of students, bring to the college classroom. The definitions we bring, based largely on our prior experiences in education, guide our behavior. When faculty and students disagree on those definitions, tensions are likely to arise and students may penalize faculty for the disagreements in the end-of-semester course evaluations. Chapter 4 summarizes the research that illustrates the reasons talkers chose to participate in class discussion and the reasons quieter students chose not to participate.

Chapter 5 presents an overview of the burgeoning scholarship regarding online courses, discussion forums in online and hybrid courses, and online discussion forums as a part of face-to-face courses. I compare synchronous and asynchronous discussion forums online and review the research concerning the effectiveness of online discussions. How does one avoid the problems of civil attention, the consolidation of responsibility, and differing definitions of the course in the online context? What are some strategies for using discussion as an online supplement in a face-to-face course and for discussion in a course that is taught entirely online?

Chapter 6 addresses several conundrums related to discussion as a classroom pedagogical strategy. We consider the issue of grading participation in discussion—a topic about which there is a surprising amount of commentary in the literature. We examine the argument against grading students' participation in classroom discussion before moving to the argument in favor of grading and proposing strategies for effective grading. I also provide a variety of approaches and strategies for grading participation in discussion. Additionally, we address the issue of helping students identify key points and the learning that is occurring in discussion. Students are often more comfortable with and more easily able to identify key information in lectures than in discussion. Recognizing important learning outcomes in discussion is a skill instructors often must facilitate in students. Finally, Chapter 6 provides some research-based insights on balancing coverage of content, student learning, and discussion.

This book has several goals, many of which are related to the challenges described in the scenario at the beginning of the chapter. The first is to answer the "why bother" question by equipping you with a research-based understanding of the value of classroom discussion for increasing student learning. I also hope to provide you with an appreciation of classroom norms that can undermine the effectiveness of discussion and strategies for how to overcome them by redefining your classroom with your students and thereby avoiding attempts at discussion that fall flat. A third goal is to empower you with strategies for keeping discussions focused, productive, and on topic. Given the increasing prevalence of online learning, this book also introduces the ways in which discussion can be utilized in an online course or moved online to supplement learning in a face-to-face course. Another goal is to introduce you to both sides of the debate over whether to grade students' participation in discussion. A final goal is to help you equip students to understand what they are achieving through discussion and to maximize that learning.

2

Is Anyone Really Paying Attention?

Today was another one of those puzzling days in class. The students seemed to be paying attention and following along with at least muted interest as you presented material. Heads were nodding. Light chuckles came in response to those bits of humor you included here and there. Some students even made fleeting eye contact as they scribbled away in their notebooks. All seemed well. That is until you asked a question about the reading assigned for the day's topic. The initial question was friendly enough—asking simply for students' perspectives. You were not asking for a rigorous analysis of the evidence. You were not asking the question in order to find out who was and wasn't prepared. It should have been easy for students who were following the lecture and who had completed the reading assignment to offer a comment or venture to take a position. Really, they didn't even have to have finished the reading in order to participate. The in-class presentation alone should have given them a basis for offering a comment or two.

Yet, when you asked the question, instead of engagement, you got disengagement. Suddenly no one would establish eye contact with you. Many busied themselves writing down something—was it the question? Not a single student volunteered an opinion. After what seemed like a long stretch of uncomfortable silence, you call on a couple of students. They seem offended that you've called on them and their body language is clear. They don't want to participate. When you ask about their views, the first mumbled, "I don't know" and the second said, "I agree with the author."

Disappointed and frustrated, you give up and you make the link between the point just made in the presentation and the reading assignment. It quickly becomes obvious that few, if any, students have completed the reading as again no one volunteers to speak. You offer some comments, followed by leading questions in hopes of sparking students' recall of the reading—still nothing. Your composure begins to slip and your irritation starts to show. "Has anyone read the assignment?" The sullen looks you get in response to the question suggest this is not a way to win friends on the end-of-semester course evaluations. Your students may be upset with you at the moment, but you are upset with them, too! They had seemed to be engaged. They seemed to be connected as you presented. Everything was fine until you probed beneath the surface a bit. Where did it all go wrong?

In this chapter, I first explain how students demonstrate civil attention and why they are able to get away with only paying civil attention. Then we focus on strategies that encourage student engagement by ensuring that students, not the faculty member, are doing most of the work. Because, as sociologists point out, the classroom is a negotiated social setting; instructors are not stuck with civil attention as the operative classroom norm. We can, beginning on the first day of class, establish new norms, strengthen students' confidence for participation, and choose to engage in behaviors in class that foster a safe emotional environment that facilitates learning and the development of critical thinking skills through student engagement.

Creating the Appearance of Paying Attention

As we know, appearances can be deceiving. The students in the scenario described above looked like they were paying attention. But perhaps that's all they were doing—creating the appearance of paying attention, or what sociologists refer to as *civil attention*. As we noted in Chapter 1, Karp and Yoels (1976) first identified this college classroom norm in the middle 1970s. In the vast majority of college classrooms, we expect college students to pay civil attention. Actually paying attention is optional.

How do students go about paying civil attention—creating the appearance of paying attention without actually having to pay attention? They do this in both the ways they act and do not act in class. A student who is reading the newspaper in the back row is not paying civil attention. The same is true for a student using his or her laptop computer to comment on posts on Facebook, to shop, to check sports scores from the previous day, or to read email. When students are texting in class or having a whispered conversation with their neighbor while the instructor is speaking, they are failing to pay civil attention. Very often faculty members have specific policies in their syllabi banning such behaviors. As faculty, we find such behaviors to be impolite, distracting, and even downright offensive. Most students accept that they are not supposed to engage in behaviors of this sort during class and therefore will at least attempt to be covert when they engage in them.

Students demonstrate civil attention not only by what they don't do, but also by the behaviors they actively display. These behaviors create the impression of paying attention; however, while we as faculty see them as signals of paying attention, we cannot know with certainty that a given student is focused on the class. For example, in order to display civil attention a student needs to be facing the faculty member with his eyes open and making occasional, fleeting eye contact with the instructor. It's important for our civil attention–paying student to make only fleeting eye contact because prolonged eye contact invites interaction, which could result in the student being called up to answer a question or provide a comment. Students also display civil attention by writing. As faculty, we assume they are taking notes on our erudite presentations. But they could be making a grocery list or merely doodling. Chuckling in response to the faculty member's attempt to inject some levity into the lecture is also a way of demonstrating civil attention. Nodding of the head as the professor speaks is yet another. As long as students are demonstrating civil attention through these and similar behaviors, faculty members are generally willing to believe that they are actually paying attention and actively listening.

How Do Students "Get Away" with Only Paying Civil Attention?

Is it safe to assume students are paying attention? Karp and Yoels (1976) suggest it is a risky assumption because in the typical college classroom students can get away with merely paying civil attention. As faculty members we must recognize our own culpability in this arrangement. While it is certainly true that students can be cognitively engaged and actively listening in class without having to participate in discussion, it is quite likely that at numerous points in the course of a class session even the most well-intentioned student will slip from paying attention into paying civil attention.

Faculty Overreliance on Lecture

This is true for a variety of reasons. The most obvious reason is our overreliance on lecture as a pedagogical strategy. I am not a person who thinks lecture is always a poor pedagogical practice. There are times when a lecture, hopefully brief and targeted, is the best way to provide necessary background or introduce new concepts and perspectives. But our overuse of lecture leads students to see the college classroom as an unfocused setting for interaction rather than a focused setting (Karp and Yoels 1976). In a focused setting, everyone is expected to participate and contribute to the interaction. In an unfocused setting, one may choose to participate or not to participate. In an unfocused setting there is no obligation for active participation in the activities of the group. Because lecture centers attention on the instructor, students rightly think that it is the instructor who has the responsibility to keep the class session moving along. Students come to see their own participation in a lecture-oriented class as optional; they may participate at appropriate times if they chose to do so, but they are not obligated to do so. It is an unfocused interaction. Faculty members tend to define the classroom differently than do students. We perceive the classroom as a focused interaction; we see participation as part of every student's responsibilities. However, our behaviors—such as making lecture the dominant pedagogical strategy—communicate something else to our students.

Fear of Direct Questioning

Another reason college students are frequently able to get away with only paying civil attention is our reluctance to use direct questioning, that is, calling on an individual student who has not verbally or nonverbally signaled to us that she is willing to be called upon. This is quite different from high school. I remember a high school teacher who would begin a class with a question about the assigned reading. Then, as a check to see who had completed the reading assignment, she would scan the room looking for students who were avoiding eye contact (in hopes of not being called upon) and then call upon gaze-averting students. If the student had not read the assignment, being embarrassed in front of the teacher and the rest of the class could be sufficient motivation to make sure he or she read the assignment in the future. Even if you were not the person being embarrassed in this manner, the implied threat that it could be you the next time provided motivation for reading the assignment. However, in the college classroom professors prefer to assume that students are adults and not to treat them like wayward children. After all, students are not compelled by law to attend college. It is a matter of choice. In fact, our students (or their parents) are paying a lot of their hard-earned money for the privilege of being in our class. So we prefer to let students assume responsibility for their own preparation for class and their own decision of whether they wish to participate in class discussions. Therefore, only rarely do we call upon students who have not volunteered to respond.

Of course, there are exceptions. Very often in language courses and mathematics courses, for example, instructors adopt pedagogies that require students to speak out as they practice pronunciations and conjugating verbs or solving homework problems and troublesome equations. Several studies of student participation in discussion in college classes put the percentage of interactions produced through direct questioning of individual students at 15 percent or less (Howard and Baird 2000; Howard and Henney 1998; Howard, Short, and Clark 1996). Even when we are willing to move away from lecture and adopt more active learning strategies, most college faculty members are still reluctant to directly call upon students who are not volunteering to participate. Dallimore, Hertenstein, and Platt's (2004) investigation of two MBA accounting courses provides a strong endorsement of "cold calling" of students in an effort to create a more democratic classroom by increasing the range of students participating. The graduate students in the study suggested that requiring and grading discussion along with directly calling upon students increased the quality of participation. However, at the undergraduate level, with students who are often less focused and motivated, cold calling can be easily perceived as a hostile act by the professor.

Students as Customers

Another factor that contributes to civil attention in college classrooms is the notion of students as "customers." The student-as-customer analogy makes sense when it comes to providing students with support services such as financial aid, internship and career placement, technology support, food service, and so on. Nonetheless it is a dangerous analogy when it comes to the classroom experience. In our capitalist society, not only is the customer always right, but one should never make the customer uncomfortable. Calling upon a student who does not wish to participate certainly makes him uncomfortable. In a study that included interviews with students who did not routinely participate in class discussion, my research colleague and I (Howard and Baird 2000) found that these quiet students would often invoke the student-as-customer analogy to justify their lack of participation. The students argued that through their tuition payment they had "purchased" the right to be silent in class if they so choose and that the instructor is the one who is being paid to participate—not the students. Weimer (2014) suggests that one reason we struggle to get students to respond to each other's comments is that they don't value other students' input. In a student-as-customer mode of thinking, it is only the faculty member who has the expert knowledge that should be valued. Therefore, students safely can ignore the input of other students. If faculty members, or administrators, adopt the student-as-customer analogy, it can lead to unwillingness to require students' active participation in class, thus encouraging the norm of civil attention.

The One Doing the Work Is the One Doing the Learning

The difficulty with a lecture-focused class without clear expectations for student engagement is that it is the faculty member who is doing most of the work in the course. Terry Doyle, author of *Helping Students Learn in a Learner-Centered Environment* (2008), argues that the basic finding of recent mind, brain, and education research is that it is the one who does the work who does the learning. So our challenge as faculty members is to change the nature of our classrooms from one wherein the professor is the person doing the majority of the work to one wherein students are doing the majority of the work. After all, we are already content experts in our fields. We're not the ones who need to learn the most.

Our challenge as faculty members is to get students to do the majority of the work through high-impact practices (see, for example, Biggs 2012). An abundance of recent scholarship points to the importance of engaging students both inside and outside of the classroom in order to facilitate learning (see, for example, Ambrose, Bridges, DiPietro, Lovett, and Norman 2010; Kuh, Kinzie, Schuh, and Witt 2005; Svinicki 2004). High-impact practices demand that students frequently interact with both faculty members and other students in substantive ways (Sidelinger 2010). Obviously, the first and most important setting for that interaction is in the classroom. To achieve the substantive interaction we desire we must overcome the norm of civil attention.

Negotiating a New Norm in Your Classroom

As in all social contexts, the college classroom is a negotiated social setting (Auster and MacRone 1994). Both with and without our awareness, we engage in a negotiation with our students to define the nature of our classrooms. Together with our students, we come to the negotiation with years of experience in similar environments and other classrooms. We do not start from scratch. Students' educational experiences both in other college courses and during their high school years profoundly shape their ideas of what our classroom should be. If paying civil attention has proven to be the norm in other courses, students' default position is likely that civil attention will be sufficient for all classrooms. Therefore, it is necessary to redefine the classroom setting and its associated norms beginning on the first day of class.

The most important factor in overcoming the norm of civil attention is how often the faculty member is engaged in interaction with students (Auster and MacRone 1994). Subject matter expertise is a necessary ingredient for student learning as it builds credibility with students; however, it is not sufficient. The most effective teaching occurs when instructor credibility (disciplinary expertise) is combined with student–faculty interaction (Pogue and AhYun 2006).

Learning Students' Names

Auster and MacRone (1994) point to four strategies for changing students' definitions of the classroom setting. First, they suggest calling on students by name when they volunteer. Of course, this implies that you have to work at learning students' names. There are a variety of ways to do this. Given that most students will voluntarily sit in the same seat each class period, you can make a seating chart to help you as you are working on learning names. If you cannot recall a student's name, you can quickly glance at the seating chart for help. Another strategy is to bring card stock and markers to class on the first day. Have students fold the card stock in half to make a nameplate and write their names in large, easy-to-read lettering. Ask students to bring their nameplates to class each day and display them until you learn everyone's name. You can also collect the nameplates at the end of each class period and then have students find their nameplates at the start of the following class period as a means of taking attendance without spending time in class doing so.

Many universities now have systems in place that allow an instructor to print a class roster that includes students' ID photos. This can be used to learn students' names. If a roster that includes students' photos is not available, another strategy is to have students come to the front of the room in small groups of two or three and write their names on the board. Take a photo of the students standing next to their names using the camera on your phone. This will allow you to practice matching faces and names outside of class. You can review the pictures on your phone whenever you have a few minutes while standing in line at the grocery store or waiting for your lunch order at the fast-food restaurant. If your class size allows it, you can also work at learning students' names during introductions on the first day of class by asking everyone to take a few seconds to introduce themselves to the class.

After each student speaks, go back and repeat the names of everyone who has already introduced him- or herself. Students will help you out if you forget a few along the way, but they also will be very appreciative that you are making an intentional effort to learn their names. You can arrive early for the next class and review students' names as they come into the room.

Again, students will forgive you for forgetting some names when they see you are working hard to get to know them as individuals. You can even challenge the class to see if they can learn all of their classmates' names at the same time you do. A few points of extra credit or a bite-size candy bar to those who can do it can provide a fun incentive for students.

Responding with Positive Reinforcement

A second strategy for changing students' definitions of the classroom and the attendant norms recommended by Auster and MacRone (1994) is to respond to students' comments and questions with positive reinforcement. If you want students to be willing to participate, you have to make it safe for them to do so. This means showing appreciation for their efforts even when they are sometimes off track. Nothing will shut down student participation more quickly or more effectively than a response to a student that seems harsh. If students perceive that you are responding harshly or embarrassing another student, they will refuse to participate, perhaps for the rest of the semester.

When a student is on the right path, simple and enthusiastic affirmations like "exactly," "that's good," or "very helpful" will go a long way to ensure continued participation. If the student is in the ballpark but needs to push his or her idea to a deeper level, you can ask follow-up questions, perhaps even leading questions that identify underlying assumptions being made by the student (e.g., "So, are you suggesting this is always the case, or do you mean only under certain circumstances?"). If the student gets stuck, you can always say something along the lines of "Josh has gotten us started on the right path here. Who can add to what he has said to help us take the next step and explore the idea a bit more?" In this manner you are taking the pressure off of Josh by calling on his peers to come to his aid. You avoid embarrassing Josh, even giving him credit and acknowledgment for providing a starting point while still challenging the class to dig into the issue more deeply. By calling upon other students to add to Josh's comments, you are also making students "do most of the work" of learning in the classroom.

There will be times, however, when the student is simply wrong or seemingly far off-base. In the latter case, it's a good practice to admit that you don't see the connection between the student's comment and the question you asked. Sometimes the student will have skipped two or three steps in the verbalizations of her thinking and being asked to explain how she got to her conclusion can help you see the connections. This may be a chance to say, "That's intriguing, but it is taking us off on a bit of a tangent. For the sake of clarity, let me try to bring us back to the topic at hand. If you'd like to explore your idea more, I'd be happy to chat with you individually about it at the end of class." If the answer is one that is simply incorrect, you can ask about how the student came to that conclusion and help the student and rest of the class identify where the misstep or mistake in thinking occurred. It helps to offer conciliatory comments such as "I can see how easy it would be to make that connection, but ..." or "That is a common mistake. I'm sure you're not the only one in class to fall into that trap. Here's how you avoid it. ..." The goal is to affirm the student's effort at providing an answer while also being clear that an error has occurred.

Positive reinforcement is necessary for creating a safe classroom environment wherein students are willing to risk being wrong. This is true whether the students' responses are on track, somewhat off track, or completely in error.

Asking Good Questions

The questions you ask when you want to engage students in discussion are also very important for facilitating student participation. Auster and MacRone (1994) rightly advise the use of analytical, instead of factual, questions and allowing sufficient time for students to respond. For example, asking "Where did Lee surrender to Grant to bring an end to the Civil War?" is a factual question for which there is only a single correct answer. It's not a good way to launch a discussion. It is much better to ask an analytical question: Why did Lee finally decide to surrender at Appomattox Court House? Was it simply due to the army being trapped, or were there other factors that contributed to the decision? The analytical question requires an examination of the topic from a variety of perspectives and numerous issues need to be addressed in order to respond fully to the question. There are multiple contributing factors, so it makes for a much better discussion than a factual question with a single correct answer. But what about disciplines like mathematics and, often, the sciences, where there is only a single correct answer? In those cases, it's best to make your questions about the process of finding the correct answer. You can ask students, How did you go about solving this equation? What steps did you use and in what order? Is this the most efficient or effective way to get to the correct answer? By asking students to describe the steps used to find an answer, they are providing you a window into their thinking that allows you to see what is clearly understood and what needs further explanation.

A safe way to get students to warm to participation is to ask opinion questions—questions for which there is no wrong answer. However, we do students a disservice if we leave them thinking that everything is simply a matter of opinion and that all opinions are equally valid. Some opinions have the weight of evidence and logic to support them. Other opinions may be based upon misunderstanding, misinformation, or personal biases. So the second step when using opinion-based questions is to help students see that opinions need to be supported with evidence and then evaluated on the basis of that evidence. This is a small step toward teaching higher-order thinking skills such as analysis, evaluation, and synthesis. A literature professor can ask students to provide their interpretation of a poem such as Gertrude Stein's "A Carafe" from her book *Tender Buttons* (1997). But the interpretation needs to be justified by and based upon the text of the poem itself and perhaps an understanding of the personal and social context in which the poem was written. Students need to be able to provide a text-based justification for their interpretation of the poem. All interpretations of the poem are not equally valid, just as not all opinions are equally valid.

Allowing Students Time to Formulate Their Thoughts

Being willing to wait for students to respond is one of the most difficult things for an instructor to do. A few seconds of uncomfortable silence in the classroom often feels like an eternity. Silence in the classroom can be a good thing if during that silence students are contemplating the topic or question at hand (Dailey 2014). We need to remember that many of our students are encountering the topics we are addressing for the first time. While we are likely intimately familiar with the subject matter we teach, our students are not. We can formulate ideas, reflections, and questions relatively quickly, but it does not come so readily to our students. They need time to consider and gather their thoughts before they are ready to speak up in class. Prefacing our questions with statements like "Take a moment and consider . . ." or "Think about (how, what, why) for a moment . . ." (Dailey 2014) is a simple step toward encouraging contemplation. The tried-and-true classroom assessment technique, the "Minute Paper" (Angelo and Cross 1993, 30), is another very helpful strategy. While originally designed as an end-of-class-period reflective exercise, the strategy can be used to launch discussions during class. Begin by providing students with an analytical question for discussion, but before starting the conversation allow students one minute to write their thoughts on the topic. As students are writing they are also developing and organizing their views. After having 60 seconds to prepare they are now ready to engage in a more meaningful, thoughtful discussion. This strategy also provides the instructor with greater freedom to use direct questioning of students because each student now has something written down to which he or she can refer if called upon. It also allows the shy and quieter students a chance to consider what they have to contribute prior to being called upon, thus making participation much safer for them.

Setting a New Norm on the First Day of Class

In order to set a norm in your classroom and overcome the norm of civil attention, it is essential to begin on the first day of class. Fassinger (1997) points out that classes are groups and that groups very quickly develop group norms. In her research, Fassinger (1997) found that the variable that best explained student participation was a student trait—confidence—not anything to do with the professor's interpersonal style. She advises that faculty can impact the structure of their classes in ways that increase students' confidence and that lead to greater participation.

Structuring Your Classroom to Facilitate Effective Discussion

Admittedly there are limits to how much a faculty member can influence the structure of his classes; for example, class-size limits are likely beyond the control of the faculty member. Still an instructor can do things that make a large class feel smaller, such as putting students into small groups for discussion of specific questions and then having each group report back to the class as a whole. Many quieter students who are reluctant to speak out in a class of 70, 40, or even 20 peers are willing to participate in a discussion with 5 to 8 classmates. Providing opportunities for students to improve their grades through participation is a structural change within the control of the faculty member (Fassinger 1997). By giving credit for participation, the instructor is signaling to students that discussion should be taken seriously and is something that will promote the learning of both the student speaking as well as his or her classmates.

Communicate that Discussion Matters

Despite an instructor's emphasis on the value of participation for facilitating learning, grading discussion is not a cure-all. In a study of six large undergraduate courses, Foster et al. (2009) compared the participation of students in sessions where students earned points for participation with participation in sessions where no points were given for participation. They found that nearly 40 percent of low-responding students in the no-points class sessions also did not participate in the sessions where participation was rewarded with points. While grading participation resulted in 60 percent of the low-responding students joining in discussion, we should also be concerned with the nearly 40 percent of low-responding students who continued to avoid all verbal participation in the classroom—even when it was a part of the course grade.

One way to address the other 40 percent's reluctance to participate in discussion is to remember that all participation need not necessarily be in the context of whole-class discussion. Students can participate in small groups or even in pairs as well as through whole-class discussions. By providing opportunities for students to interact with each other (not merely with the instructor), the faculty member is creating bonds of acquaintance and friendship that will facilitate further participation and greater learning. This leads to a positive emotional climate in the classroom wherein students are more likely to develop the confidence necessary to participate in discussion.

Build Student Confidence Early in the Semester

While Fassinger (1997) concludes that it is student confidence, rather than faculty interpersonal style, that most influences participation in discussion, a faculty member can seek to increase participation through activities that build student confidence early in the semester. One approach for the first day of class is giving students a quiz over the syllabus. Put students into small groups of five or so and provide them with a list of questions that are answered in the syllabus: Which books must you buy? How many exams will there be in this course? What is the policy for late work? Where is the professor's office? What are her office hours? Students complete the quiz in small groups and each group turns in a single sheet with all group members' names on it. This exercise serves two purposes: familiarizing students with the syllabus and developing a positive emotional climate as students begin to get to know each other as they work collaboratively. While everyone is expected to get 100 percent of the points on this quiz, it establishes the norm that discussions are important and valuable and therefore merit being rewarded with credit. It also communicates that the instructor will not be the person doing all the work in this course. Students will be expected to be responsible for their own learning and understanding.

Be Explicit about the Importance of Discussion for Learning

When making participation in discussion a part of students' grades (and even when it is not a part of the course grade), it is important to have a conversation with students about the importance of discussion for student learning. As we noted in Chapter 1, because the research evidence demonstrates that students both learn more and develop critical thinking skills through participation in discussion, we include it as a course requirement. Providing students with an explanation of why we structure our course to include expectations for significant participation in discussion on the first day helps to change students' understandings of norms for the course. We will return to the topic of whether and how to grade students' participation in discussion in Chapter 6.

The Reciprocal Interview: A First-Day Activity

Another first-day-of-class strategy for changing classroom norms is known as the *reciprocal interview* (Hermann and Foster 2008). In this approach the instructor begins by interviewing students regarding their goals and expectations about the course. Inevitably, the initial goal expressed may be to "get an A," but with practice the instructor can prompt students to think about what they hope to learn and the skills they hope to develop in the course. Do they see the course as contributing knowledge or skills that will benefit them in their future careers? Do they expect the course to be difficult or relatively easy for them and why? Then, in turn, the students have the opportunity to interview the professor regarding his or her expectations for the course. What does the professor expect of students? What does A-level work look like in this class? What does the professor hope students will take away from the course?

The next step in the reciprocal interview is for the instructor to ask students about what they expect of the professor in the class. Students will inevitably begin to list such things as "I expect you to be on time," "I expect you to be prepared for class," "I expect you to treat students fairly," and "I expect you will do your part to help me learn." Then after affirming the appropriateness of these expectations and pledging to do the best one can to fulfill them, the instructor can turn the expectations around. "Just as you expect me to be on time, I expect you to arrive to class on time." "Just as you expect me to be prepared for class, I expect you to be prepared for class." "Just as you expect me to be fair with you, I expect you to treat me fairly by being honest, doing your own work, and putting forth your best effort." "Just as you expect me to help you learn I expect you to also accept responsibility for your own learning. I will do my part to help you learn, but you must do your part as well." Frank exchanges like these on the first day of class can fundamentally alter students' expectations for a course and the concurrent class-room norms. Hermann and Foster's (2008) reciprocal interview can also reduce classroom incivility and create a safe environment by making expectations for behavior explicit.

This is also an opportune moment to address the issue of students as customers in the classroom. When the student-as-customer analogy comes up in my courses, I respond with another analogy. If the student is a customer, then the instructor is the academic equivalent of a physical fitness trainer. The fitness trainer is not paid to make the customer "happy" and to never make the customer uncomfortable. In fact, it is quite the opposite. The job of a physical trainer is to push the customer to achieve at levels that were not previously possible. This will involve a lot of challenge and perhaps even some pain. If your academic trainer, your instructor, is not pushing you out of your comfort zone and not challenging you to do more academically than you think you are capable of achieving, then you are not getting your money's worth out of the exchange. This tends to cause students to see the notion of being a customer in a different light.

Guided Notes

Guided notes (Heward 1994) are another strategy for overcoming the norm of civil attention. We know that even the most well-intentioned students can and do lose focus during a class and especially during a lecture-based class. Guided notes are handouts prepared by the instructor that include partial lecture notes or an incomplete lecture outline that students use to take notes during class. Guided notes can make the organization of a lecture more obvious to students and encourage them to follow along. Guided notes can be aligned with PowerPoint slides and provide an alternative to making copies of the slides available to students. Many instructors worry, often based on their personal experience, that when PowerPoint slides are available to students on a course management website, students will take that as a license to skip attending class. Guided notes provide part of the information contained on the PowerPoint slides, but students must be present to complete the information by taking notes. Students must actively listen or they risk having incomplete notes at the end of the class session. Guided notes also have the potential to improve students' note-taking skills as they learn to identify important information in the lecture. And students have to be truly paying attention, not merely paying civil attention, in order to complete the guided notes. This means students are more likely to be engaged and to ask questions in class. Heward (1994) found that students' exam scores improved with the use of guided notes. They also have the advantage of forcing faculty members to carefully and thoughtfully organize our lectures, which can also lead to increased student learning.

Get Closer to Students

Research has shown (see, for example, Howard, Zoeller, and Pratt 2006) that students who speak up most frequently during class discussion are disproportionately seated in the front third of the classroom. Their location makes it easy for you to always call upon these talkative students during class discussions. Being in the front of the room, near the instructor, also encourages these students to pay attention rather than limit themselves to civil attention, while the more quiet students and those who would rather pay only civil attention sit further away from you. So, if those students won't come to you, you should go to them. Move around the room as much as the physical arrangement of classroom furniture allows. If you can walk up and down the aisles as you present material, do so. As you get closer to those students in the back corner, their level of attention will increase. Then, if you ask for student input while standing in the back of the room, those students are more likely to volunteer to participate. The same is true when you put students in small groups. As you wander between groups and listen to their discussions they are more likely to stay on topic. They are also more likely to ask for your assistance if they are unclear about the charge to the group or get stuck in their problem solving. If the rows are too tightly packed to allow you to move up and down them, you can still get out from behind the podium and move side-to-side across the front of the room. While not as ideal as being able to move to the back of the room, the side-to-side movement can help refocus students' attention and therefore improve their level of participation in discussion.

Talk with Students Outside of Class

Weaver and Qi (2005) in their study of students at a large state university campus found that interaction with instructors outside of class is positively associated with students' participation in class. Increasing the quality and frequency of student–faculty interactions both inside and outside of the classroom has been nearly universally affirmed (see Braxton, Eimers, and Bayer 1996, 607). The lesson of this work is that faculty should both create and take advantage of opportunities to interact with students outside of class. Make it a requirement that all students come for a two-minute visit during your office hours twice during a semester—if for no other reason than to give you an opportunity to get to know them and learn their names. You can also use these meetings as an opportunity to check in with students who are struggling in the course and ask about their study approaches. If you see students at the campus food court, in the stands at the game, or at the local grocery store, greet them even when you cannot remember their name. Perhaps you will recall their name as you chat for a few seconds. If not, you call always plead that you have trouble remembering names when students are out of the classroom context and ask them to remind you of their name. Weaver and Qi (2005) have documented that these out-of-class interactions can have a significant payoff in terms of students' willingness to engage in discussion during class.

How Instructor Behavior Impacts Student Participation

While Fassinger's (1996, 1997) research did not find instructor characteristics to have as significant or direct of an impact on student participation in discussion as did student characteristics and class structure, numerous researchers have pointed to a variety of instructor traits or practices that can directly or indirectly impact students' willingness to participate. Therefore in addition to taking steps to build students' confidence, we need to take a close look at what we can do to facilitate classroom interaction. Students' willingness to participate in discussion is related to perceptions of the instructor and the classroom environment (Myers and Claus 2012). Sagayadevan and Jeyaraj (2012) found a link between emotional engagement and student learning. How can instructors create an emotional environment that facilitates student learning? What instructor behaviors lead to student perceptions that either inhibit or encourage class discussion? How can we create a classroom environment that encourages students' emotional engagement, participation, and learning?

Instructor Aggressiveness Restricts Participation

Myers and Rocca (2001) concluded that instructor aggressiveness is a significant deterrent to student participation. However, they make an important distinction between instructor argumentativeness (defending a position and refuting another) and instructor aggressiveness (attacking another person). The former did not adversely impact classroom climate while the latter was negatively related to classroom climate. Students' perceptions of instructor aggressiveness inhibit participation in discussion. This is likely why a faculty member who enjoys a "bare-knuckled fight" over competing perspectives will often have difficulty getting students to respond with much enthusiasm. In many ways, this is akin to the stereotypical musclebound beach bully kicking sand in the face of the 98-pound weakling. It's simply not a fair fight. The faculty member has years of graduate study as well as years of teaching the subject behind him. The students are encountering the subject likely for the first time. Students are certainly smart enough to know they are at a serious disadvantage when it comes to an intellectual brawl with the instructor over competing perspectives in the instructor's discipline. Therefore, they take the safe path and avoid participating in the argument altogether. Who can blame them? While the instructor may be aiming for argumentativeness, students may perceive it as aggressiveness.

For such a strategy to be effective, rather than setting up an instructor-versus-students argument, it would be much better to structure it as a debate between students who either choose or are assigned perspectives to defend. It is important to provide time for students to gather information and fashion their arguments. You can do this by requiring students to complete a short writing assignment identifying the strengths and potential weaknesses of their assigned perspective. Then they come to class after having spent some time reflecting on the perspective and, should they have trouble "thinking on their feet" during class, they can refer to their paper for help. Alternatively, this could be a group debate with students in small groups collectively formulating their arguments regarding the strengths of their assigned perspective and the potential weaknesses of other perspectives prior to the larger group debate regarding the competing perspectives. It is always a good idea to remind students upfront of the ground rule that it is positions that are being challenged and questioned, not individuals. So it is acceptable to say, "That's logically inconsistent." It is not permissible to say, "Only a naïve person could support that position." This approach allows for argumentativeness (defending a position and refuting another) while avoiding aggressiveness (attacking another person). It also makes for a fair fight over the competing perspectives as students have similar levels of exposure to and understanding of the topic. It is no longer the beach bully versus the 98-pound weakling.

While it is aggressiveness rather than argumentativeness that inhibits students' participation in class discussion, argumentativeness still requires a deft hand. While many faculty members enjoy playing devil's advocate in order to bring out implicit assumptions in a student's position or to help students recognize the logical outcome of an approach they are advocating, students easily perceive argumentativeness as aggressiveness. So how might we minimize the risk associated with argumentativeness? One strategy is to be clear that you are adopting the role of devil's advocate by explicitly saying so. This can help students understand that you are not necessarily disagreeing with their position, but are asking them to justify and defend it. If you teach on a campus where students are often very liberal, you might ask the class, "How would a good political conservative respond to your claim? How might they see the issue differently? Does that different view have merit?" It can also help to depersonalize the issue when taking the devil's advocate approach. You can say, "Audrey has very clearly outlined for us the classic 'conservative' position on this issue. But I want you to now assume that you are a political liberal. How are you going to respond to the claims of the conservative viewpoint? What counterarguments can you make?" This approach does several things. It takes away any perception that this is the instructor attacking a student or that only politically correct perspectives (be they liberal or conservative) are allowed in the classroom. It also depersonalizes the issue. We are not so much critiquing Audrey's perspective as we are the conservative (liberal, Marxist, classical, neoclassical, modernist, postmodernist, etc.) position. Students don't feel as if they are attacking a classmate (and thereby making oneself vulnerable to a counterattack) should they offer a different view. Finally, it engages the students in playing the role of the devil's advocate even if they personally agree with Audrey's position. By making the students do the work, instead of the instructor doing the work, students will learn more.

Creating a Safe Environment for Participation

Sidelinger and Booth-Butterfield (2010) recommend instructors first create opportunities for student-to-student connectedness and only afterwards move toward initiating student participation. They point out that positive student-to-student connectedness is associated with increased student involvement regardless of class size. Therefore, early in the semester, instructors need to create opportunities for students to collaboratively work together. In courses with homework assignments, this can be accomplished by giving students the opportunity to review their homework with a classmate or a small group (Bean and Peterson 1998). For problems where students came to different answers, they have to work together to figure out which is the correct response (if either). Such examinations of the logic of their work will inevitably improve learning. It also establishes the norm that students can learn from each other, not just from the professor, and the norm that everyone has something to contribute to their classmates' learning.

Another way to encourage student-to-student engagement is to provide a question to the class, be it multiple choice or open-ended, and allow students to work in pairs to determine an answer. Instructors can then use student response systems ("clickers") to check the class's understanding. A less technology-intensive approach is to provide students with cards that have A, B, C, or D on them and ask students to hold up the card indicating their answer. The card approach has the advantage of avoiding the anonymity embedded in a student response system. The instructor can quickly see if pairs of students differed from the rest of the class and follow up with them. The opportunity to work with a classmate or classmates on problems builds positive bonds between students that will pay off later in a greater willingness to engage in discussion.

Another step faculty members can take to encourage a positive emotional climate is the use of self-disclosure. Cayanus (2004), in his review of the research on self-disclosure in the college classroom, found that students take a more active role when teachers talk about themselves in courses than in courses where teachers did not talk about themselves. But self-disclosure can be tricky. It is easy to overdo it, leaving students thinking that you'd rather talk about your personal life than the subject matter at hand. Cayanus (2004) recommends that as you organize your lecture, you pick appropriate spots for self-disclosure. Can you tell a cute story about when your son was two years old to illustrate a childhood development theory? Would nursing students better grasp the importance of a particular treatment modality if you explained how you learned it on-the-job at the hospital? Self-disclosure is most effective when it is relevant to the material. While students might enjoy knowing which movie you went to see over the weekend, criminology students benefit more if you describe something that occurred in the movie which illustrates a misperception about crime and criminals. In a political science course, it may be appropriate to talk about the "get out the vote" strategies utilized in a political campaign for which you volunteered as an undergraduate. It helps to vary the topics of self-disclosure; students will tire of hearing about your show horses particularly if they are not relevant to the course. It is also a good idea to vary the timing of self-disclosure to maintain interest. Self-disclosure anecdotes can be used as a story to begin a class session or to introduce a topic mid-class or as a way of reaffirming an important point at the end of class. As an added benefit, positive, honest, and relevant faculty self-disclosure is associated with more positive evaluations of the instructor (Lannutti and Strauman 2006).

Faculty and Student Similarity (or Not)

It is much easier for faculty to create a safe classroom environment and build positive bonds with and between students when students perceive the faculty member to be similar to them. This is known as *homophily*. Myers et al. (2009) found that students' participation was positively correlated with their perceptions of instructor social and physical attractiveness as well as perceived background and attitudinal homophily. Instructor homophily refers to the extent to which students perceive their instructors to have backgrounds, beliefs, attitudes, and values that are the same or similar to those of the students themselves.

This presents some added challenges for faculty members whose social class, race, gender, religion (or lack thereof), sexual orientation, and so forth are different from that of the majority of students. Semenza (2014) notes that as a faculty member ages, and his or her students remain 18–22 years old, it becomes increasingly difficult to connect with and relate to them. We grew up in different eras with unique popular culture experiences and at least a somewhat different social context. In an essay describing his choice of a casual classroom demeanor, which is reflected in his choice to wear informal clothing in class, Leonard (2014) recognizes that while this approach helps to create a safe emotional environment in class, as a white male he does not have to worry that his attire will cause students to question his expertise or authority. His "whiteness" authenticates his authority. In 12 years of teaching, Leonard (2014) reports students have never complained about his casual clothing or even about his occasional swearing in class. The same was not true for colleagues who are women or people of color. White males simply have an advantage is this sense. Students will take the authority and expertise of a white male for granted. This will not necessarily be the case for women or people of color.

In another essay reflecting upon the challenges of relating to students and creating a safe emotional environment, Redmond (2014), a black female professor, observes she has witnessed other black female professors "going mean" in response to students and colleagues questioning their authority or devaluing their person. Going mean involves developing a cold disposition that is also more formal and distant, for example, requiring students to address you as "Doctor" or setting strict and rigid boundaries for interacting with students.

When students perceive you as different from themselves, they are more likely to assume that one's social location as a minority or a woman is the determinant of one's viewpoint as opposed to one's expert authority. While it is possible to engage students who are different from you in significant ways, it is more difficult. And the challenge is greater for women and people of color.

It is certainly easier to relate to nontraditional students, for example, if you were a nontraditional student yourself. It's easier to understand the private, residential, liberal arts college experience of your students if you went through something quite similar yourself as an undergraduate. If you grew up in a blue-collar family and worked two jobs while attending college, it is easier for you to understand and appreciate the obstacles first-generation students in similar circumstances face and it is likely much more difficult for you to empathize with students whom you perceive as coming from backgrounds of privilege and comfort.

While we cannot change our backgrounds, our gender, our race, or our sexual orientation to become more like our students, nor would we want to, we can take steps to help our students see us as human beings with plenty in common even if our social class, religious, or racial backgrounds are different from their own. One way to become "more human" to our students is to use self-disclosure as noted earlier. While you may have grown up in an urban area and your students in a rural area, you both grew up, went to school, had siblings, and so on. You can emphasize the things you have in common in your self-disclosure. Once some relationship with students has been built through stressing commonalities, then you may be able to use stories of how, for example, it was different growing up in a blue-collar family to help your students of more privileged backgrounds appreciate the challenges faced by first-generation college students, students of color, or students from impoverished backgrounds. At this point, students are likely to find stories of how things may have been different for you when compared to them to be quite intriguing.

The findings of Myers et al. (2009) with regard to physical and social attractiveness provide some food for thought as well. On one level this seems like a very superficial concern. But there is an abundance of social research that documents that appearance matters (for a summary, see Ruane and Cerulo 2008). Appearance has a significant impact on perceptions and assumptions. In general, we tend to make positive assumptions about people who are attractive—we give attractive people the benefit of the doubt in all types of circumstances. While we cannot and should not attempt to fundamentally alter our physical appearance to foster student participation—no one is calling for plastic surgery here—it does make sense to put one's best foot forward. As trivial as it may seem, students may interpret the faculty member's care and attention given to his or her appearance as a sign of respect for them and for the classroom situation. In particular for younger faculty facing students who question their authority or expertise, it is often a good idea to take a somewhat more formal, professional (think business casual) approach to classroom attire to set oneself apart from students rather than dressing in the very casual attire often favored while in graduate school. Benton (2013) described a yearlong experiment wherein he chose to dress more formally (without, as he says, overdoing it and looking like an "administrator"). He found that dressing more formally contributed to classes running more smoothly with fewer disruptions, and fewer grade appeals, and students beginning emails with "Dear Professor" instead of "Hey." Of course, one can argue the opposite, that dressing formally stresses the barriers between faculty and students and may inhibit interaction. Regardless, the faculty member's approach to attire likely does impact the style of interaction. I encourage faculty members to experiment a bit, as did Benton (2008), to find what attire works best for you, remembering that attractiveness can help engage students even if we think it is a superficial or trivial reason for doing so.

In addition to physical attractiveness, there is also the issue of social attractiveness. Faculty who smile at their students, who laugh with their students, who are welcoming and make an effort to know students by name and learn about them as people are perceived to be more socially attractive. So if you feel you cannot be or do not want to be perceived as physically attractive, being socially attractive can help you overcome the norm of civil attention and engage students in class discussion. Fortunately, actions that facilitate social attractiveness (e.g., learning students' names) are also actions that facilitate the creation of a safe environment for discussion.

The Delicate Matter of Direct Questions

As noted before, relatively few classroom interactions occur as a result of faculty members directly calling upon students who are not volunteering to participate. College faculty members tend to agree that students are adults and should be making their own choices about how to maximize their learning. Therefore, we are reluctant to directly question students. But should we overcome our reluctance and call on individual students?

There is a long history of direct questioning in some higher education settings. For example, law schools often have a tradition of utilizing the Socratic Method—the use of probing questions in a group discussion to help expose underlying assumptions, logical conclusions, and generally to get to the most important aspects of the topic being discussed. While the Socratic Method is sometimes portrayed in popular culture as means of grilling a student or placing him on the hot-seat while seeking to expose his errors in thinking, the reality is usually much less threatening. It is more of a form of coaching and leading students to explore their own thinking by asking a series of follow-up questions. Even so, such an approach can feel very threatening, particularly to undergraduates. So what can an instructor do to make direct questioning less threatening and more beneficial for undergraduates?

One of the best ways to reduce the discomfort of direct questioning of undergraduates is to provide them with time to think and organize their views prior to calling upon them. We discussed the Minute Paper (Angelo and Cross 1993) previously. Building upon the Minute Paper is another classroom assessment technique called *Think-Pair-Share* (Angelo and Cross 1993). This is likely the most commonly used classroom assessment technique in higher education. Begin with a Minute Paper providing students with a question for them to consider. Students have 60 seconds to write down their thoughts in response to the question (Think). Then have students turn to one classmate (Pair) and reciprocally explain what they have written (Share). This strategy forces every student to interact with one other student after you have given them time to think and consider. After the paired sharing, you can directly call upon any student because they have had time to collect their thoughts before speaking and they have had an opportunity to practice articulating those thoughts with another student prior to being asked to share them with the whole class. This makes the direct questioning much less threatening.

Of course, following a Think-Pair-Share, you can ask for two or three volunteers to share their responses to check students' understanding. I prefer to ask students, "Whose partner had a particularly insightful response? I want you to 'call out' your partner and have him or her share with the class if he or she had an especially helpful insight." This has a couple of advantages. First, it is not you, the instructor, directly calling upon a student—it is a classmate doing so. And by doing so they are providing affirmation to other students that what they have to say is important and merits sharing with the entire class. This affirmation also makes the act of speaking before the whole class much less threatening. Second, this approach slows down the talkative, extroverted students who most frequently volunteer and increases the possibility that those quiet, introverted students with good insights will be called upon to share by a classmate.

Conclusion

If we do not consciously and intentionally seek to change the norms in our classrooms, we are likely to find ourselves in a situation similar to that described at the outset of this chapter, with students paying only civil attention. But we don't have to settle for civil attention. Because college classrooms are social settings where definitions of the situation are continually being negotiated, we can employ strategies that create new norms, including the expectation that all students will participate in discussion. We can take steps in the first class session of the semester that will lead to different classroom discussion norms. We can utilize strategies that build students' confidence and encourage participation. We can systematically create an emotional environment that encourages students' sense of safety and increases their engagement in class. Always our goal and our motivation is that students will learn more and develop their critical thinking skills as a result of being engaged in classroom discussion. However, civil attention is not the only classroom norm that inhibits participation in the classroom and therefore may undermine student learning. The consolidation of responsibility is yet another norm that must be addressed if we are to effectively engage students in order to promote learning and the development of critical thinking skills.

3

The Challenge of Dominant Talkers

It had been a good day. Despite the "nerves" induced by a colleague's presence in your classroom, part of a developmental peer
review of your teaching, things had gone well. Students appeared
to have read the assignment and the back-and-forth dialogue had
been great. Whenever you stopped and invited participation, there
were always three or four students who readily joined the conversation. When responses were less thorough than you hoped, you were
able to pull more in-depth responses out of the contributors with
some well-timed follow-up questions. You even noticed the quiet
students turning toward and looking at their classmates whenever
one of them spoke up. It felt good to have such a successful class
session when a peer was there to observe.

The debriefing with your colleague also went well as she noted
a variety of strengths in your teaching and affirmed your efforts in
the classroom. However, she also pointed out something troubling.
That wonderful discussion you had with the class? It turns out
that it was a dynamic discussion with only five students. Your
colleague correctly noted that the other 22 students in the class
merely observed the discussion you had with five very engaged and
insightful students. Sure, many of them appeared to be actively
listening, but they were not making comments or asking questions
of you or their classmates. They contributed nothing to their
classmates' learning and you hadn't even noticed. You completely

missed that the vast majority were silent for the entire class session—how embarrassing!

Is that what was happening in all your courses? Upon reflecting you have to admit it was—a few students doing all or most of the talking. If other hands went up, you called on them, but very few did. What can you do to break this pattern? How does one go about getting those mostly silent students engaged in the discussion? Why do some students so readily participate in discussion while others seemingly never do? How can you prevent a few students from completely dominating the class?

In this chapter I first share the findings of research into students' participation in discussion in the college classroom. Which students are most likely to accept the consolidation of responsibility and become dominant talkers? What individual characteristics, such as student gender, age, and race, and what contextual factors, such as class size and instructor gender, are correlated with students' participation in class discussion? Finally, what pedagogical strategies can help to increase the number of students who participate while limiting the dominance of the most talkative students?

Dominant Talkers and the Consolidation of Responsibility

Would it be comforting to know that you and many other professors have run into what is called the *norm of the consolidation of responsibility*? As noted in Chapter 1, this norm, first identified by Karp and Yoels (1976), means that in the typical college or university classroom, a small number of students (five to eight) will account for 75 to 95 percent of all student verbal contributions to discussion regardless of class size. Research has consistently confirmed the existence of this norm.

In a study of 15 sections of the introductory sociology course taught by nine different instructors at a large Midwestern university, my colleagues and I (Howard, Zoeller, and Pratt 2006) found that in the typical 75-minute class period there were 49 instances of student verbal participation. That's a lot of discussion going on. On average there was one student comment or question every minute and a half. I don't know about you, but if I had students speaking up every 90 seconds, my initial reaction would be that I had done a great job of engaging my students in discussion. After class I'd be patting myself on the back on the way back to my office. However, upon closer examination, we found that was not the whole story. In fact, that version of the story was quite misleading.

While there was a considerable amount of conversation taking place, not all students were participating, nor were students participating equally. In the typical class session we observed, only 12 of the 39 students present spoke up at all. That means 27 students (70% of those in attendance) never spoke during the observed class period. Of the 12 students participating in a typical class session, 6 of them spoke up only once while the other 6 accounted for 92 percent of all the student interactions (Howard, Zoeller, and Pratt 2006). Clearly, responsibility for student participation in discussion was consolidated in the hands of a few students in these courses.

Other scholars have found the norm of the consolidation of responsibility in their research as well. Relying on students' self-reports of participation, Crombie et al. (2003) in their study of over 500 students at a Canadian university found evidence for the consolidation of responsibility in that roughly one third of students were "more active" compared to "less active" students in the rest of the class. Fortney, Johnson, and Long (2001) described the dominant talkers who accept responsibility for classroom discussion as "compulsive communicators." In an observational study at a regional campus of a state university, Fritschner (2000) also confirmed the consolidation of responsibility was in operation. Sixsmith, Dyson, and Nataatmadja (2006), in focus group interviews with information technology students, also found general agreement among students that a select few class members would do all the talking if allowed.

Even in courses with relatively little discussion occurring and in courses with few students, the consolidation of responsibility is still present. In a triangulated study utilizing classroom observation, survey, and interview, Nunn (1996) found that only about 1 minute of the typical 40-minute class period was spent in student talk with roughly one quarter of students participating. In their study of a First Year Seminar course with only 15 students enrolled, Goodman, Murphy, and D'Andrea (2012) found that the students felt that a few could carry the discussion for the rest of the class while the majority of students adhered to a "norm of silence"—not perceiving themselves as obligated to participate in the conversation. The consolidation of responsibility tends to be the default setting in the college classroom, regardless of class size, unless the instructor takes intentional steps to create a new norm.

Which Students Are Most Likely to Become Dominant Talkers?

Which students are most likely to dominate participation in class discussion? Before delving into what the scholarship of teaching and learning reveals about this question, a pair of cautions is in order with regard to research on classroom discussion based on classroom observation and on students' self-reports via surveys or interviews.

Students, particularly male students, have a tendency to significantly overestimate their level of participation in class discussion. When comparing students' self-reports on surveys regarding the frequency of their participation in discussion to actual observations of the same students' interactions in class, we find that students think they are participating much more frequently than they are. Therefore the most reliable research findings regarding student participation in discussion are those that utilize both survey and observation as research methodologies. By using surveys, researchers can get a sense of students' perceptions of the course, their instructor, and their classmates as well as students' views of their own role in the class. By using observational research, scholars can check students' perceptions of participation against what is actually happening in the classroom.

Karp and Yoels (1976) defined a "talker" as a student who participated twice or more in a single class session and a "non-talker" as a student who participated only once or not at all during a class session. In my own research (with a variety of colleagues) on classroom discussion norms utilizing student self-reports of participation, I had to redefine the definition of "talkers" when observations of the same students in class revealed that students were not participating at the levels they reported (see Howard and Baird 2000; Howard, James, and Taylor 2002; Howard, Zoeller, and Pratt 2006). While this was quite surprising at first, the finding was very consistent. In each of these studies, it was male students who were most likely to overestimate their participation in discussion. For example, in one study (Howard and Baird 2000), we found that based on observation less than 8 percent of all students spoke twice or more in a given class period. However, 75 percent of these students claimed to speak up twice or more per class period in their survey self-reports and males overestimated their participation more so than did females. This tendency to significantly overestimate one's contributions to discussions makes studies that rely solely on students' self-reports via survey somewhat suspect, particularly when it comes to claims about the impact of student gender on participation. Males are more likely to overestimate their level of participation compared to females, which can lead to a perception that males dominate class discussion, which is not supported by observational evidence.

A second caution is related to instructor gender. As a general rule, in both interviews and survey responses, students will claim that instructor gender is not related to their level of participation in a course. However, observational studies have found that instructor gender often does make a difference in the amount of discussion occurring and the percentage of students participating (see, for example, Howard and Henney 1998). Keeping these cautions in mind, let's examine what the research has to say about which students are most likely to participate in discussion and what factors influence their level of participation.

Individual Characteristics and Participation in Discussion

In their study of factors that influence student participation in college classroom discussion, Crombie et al. (2003) rightly pointed out that both individual characteristics and contextual factors play a role. Individual characteristics include the student's gender, age, race, country of origin (native versus international students), and perceptions, or normative understandings, of the classroom. Contextual factors include influences that are part of the classroom environment and are controlled by someone other than the student—the instructor or university administrators. Contextual factors include class size (enrollment in the course), gender of the instructor, pedagogical strategies employed by the instructor, seating arrangement, academic disciplinary area, and course level. Of all these factors, both individual and contextual, the one to receive the greatest amount of attention in research has been student gender.

Student Gender and Participation in Discussion

The investigation of student gender as a major determinant of participation in discussion in the college classroom springs from Hall and Sandler's (1982) "chilly climate" thesis. Hall and Sandler (1982) suggested that the college classroom is an arena where the operative norms create a climate that is not as welcoming for women as it is for men. Tannen (1991) in her work on gender conversation rituals argues that male and female students define the college classroom differently and, therefore, respond to the environment differently. She points to three factors that lead to men (presumably) speaking more than women in class. First, men are more comfortable with the public nature of the classroom, while women tend to be more comfortable speaking in private settings. Second, while women tend to prefer more collaborative styles of interaction, men are more comfortable with the competitive, debate-like interaction that is often found in college classrooms. Finally, Tannen (1991) argues that men tend to define participation in, and domination of, discussion as a part of their role as students, whereas women are more likely to self-monitor and limit their participation in order to avoid dominating discussion. In essence, the argument goes, the traditional college classroom features a male interaction style and is therefore a less comfortable environment for women than it is for men.

Of course, Hall and Sandler (1982) assume that some male professors engage in overtly sexist behaviors that inhibit women's participation. And it is quite likely that professors were more likely to engage in sexist behaviors in 1982 than today. But the chilly climate can exist despite the best intentions of faculty because of the male interaction style typically found in college classrooms. However, as Tannen (1991) notes, conversational style is not absolute. Styles can and do change in response to context and to the styles utilized by other participants in the conversation. So while the traditional college classroom may have once typically featured a competitive interaction style favored by men, it is entirely possible that the norms and interaction styles typically utilized in college classrooms have changed toward a more collaborative style since Hall and Sandler (1982) first postulated their chilly climate thesis over 30 years ago.

Despite Hall and Sandler's (1982) assumption of a chilly climate and Tannen's (1991) work on gender interaction styles, the research results with regard to the influence of student gender on participation in classroom discussion have always been mixed. This is not to say that the higher education environment has never been chilly to females in other ways (e.g., incidents of sexual harassment, or disciplines wherein women are significantly underrepresented and made to feel as if they do not belong). However, there has not been a consistent finding that males dominate discussion in the college classroom at the expense of female students.

The relationship between student gender and participation in classroom discussion is a complicated one. In some studies, based on students' self-reports, researchers have found that males claim to participate more frequently than females (Auster and MacRone 1994; Crombie et al. 2003; Fassinger 1995). Karp and Yoels (1976), utilizing classroom observation of students' actual participation, also found that males participated more frequently than their female classmates. Crawford and MacLeod (1990) found that males participated more than females in the small college courses they studied, but not in the university courses examined. Pearson and West (1991), in a study of communication courses, found that females asked fewer questions than did male students and that self-reported masculinity was correlated with increased question asking. Looking at graduate students, Brooks (1982) found that males exhibited more aggressiveness, interrupting faculty and other students more frequently than did females, particularly in courses taught by female faculty.

On the other hand, numerous studies, and the vast majority of those utilizing classroom observation as a methodology (instead of relying on students' self-reports), have found no significant differences in participation by student gender (Boersma 1981; Constantinople, Cornelius, and Gray 1988; Heller, Puff, and Mills 1985; Howard and Baird 2000; Howard and Henney 1998; Howard, James, and Taylor 2002; Weaver and Qi 2005). In addition, and completely contradicting the predictions of the "chilly climate" thesis, other studies have found that female students participate at greater levels than their male counterparts. Canada and Pringle (1995) found that in mixed-sex classes, females initiated more interactions than males. Heller, Puff, and Mills (1985) found that it was female students who received the more analytical questions from the instructors while male students were more often limited to the less challenging factual questions, causing the researchers to conclude that the college classroom may be a chilly climate for men rather than for women. While Fritschner (2000) found that younger female students were the least likely demographic group to participate in discussion (compared to older females, older males, and younger males) in the mixed-age college classroom, females participated more frequently overall in comparison to males. Howard, Zoeller, and Pratt (2006) in another observational study of students in introductory sociology courses found that a higher percentage of females participated in discussion, but male talkers spoke up more frequently than female talkers. Similarly, my colleagues and I (Howard, Short, and Clark 1996) found that while a higher percentage of females participated and a higher percentage of females were talkers, male talkers spoke more often than female talkers.

Therefore, the strongest conclusion from the research on impact of student gender on participation in classroom discussion is that when relying on self-reports, male students are likely to claim that they participate more often. However, research based on observation calls the students' perceptions into doubt. There is no consistent finding regarding the impact of student gender on participation in college classroom discussion. Instructors do need to be paying attention to patterns that emerge in their classrooms. Does one gender or the other dominate discussion? Does one gender have less opportunity to contribute because members of the other gender consistently volunteer and speak up more quickly? The first step in ensuring equitable participation by student gender is being sensitive to and aware of patterns in your classroom.

Student Age and Participation in Discussion

In contrast to student gender, an individual factor that has been consistently shown to impact participation in classroom discussion is students' age. In mixed-age college classrooms, where traditional (18- to 24-year-old) students are combined with nontraditional students (25 years or older), it is the older students who speak up most frequently. In a series of studies I conducted with colleagues, nontraditional students spoke from twice as often to four times as often as their traditionally aged classmates (Howard and Baird 2000; Howard and Henney 1998; Howard, James, and Taylor 2002; Howard, Zoeller and Pratt 2006). These and other studies conclude that it is the older students who are most likely to become the dominant talkers in class (Crombie et al. 2003; Fritschner 2000; Howard, Short, and Clark 1996; Weaver and Qi 2005).

In exploring reasons for their participation via interviews, older nursing students expressed greater confidence to participate when compared to their younger classmates (Loftin, Davis, and Hartin 2010). It is quite likely that the more extensive life and professional experience of nontraditional students gives them the ability and the confidence to contribute to discussions of a much wider range of topics than do traditional 18- to 24-year-old college students. Likewise, it is often the case that nontraditional students are very goal-directed, paying their own way through college or seeking a degree in order to earn a promotion at work, and therefore are motivated to excel in all aspects of the student role. While nontraditional students who have been out of high school for a long period of time before enrolling in college may have weaker academic preparation when compared to their younger classroom peers, they are likely to make up for any deficits via their dedication, energy, and enthusiasm.

Student Race and Participation in Discussion

An under-investigated individual factor in participation in college classroom discussions is student race. Relatively few studies have actually attempted to observe and measure participation by race. In a study of introductory sociology courses at a large urban university, we (Howard, Zoeller, and Pratt 2006) found that student race did not have a statistically significant impact on participation rates. However, in our classroom observations we discovered that on certain topics, minority students became the dominant talkers for a given class period. This was true, for example, when students touched upon the topic of police profiling. The normally dominant talkers in that class session took a backseat to minority students, particularly African Americans, who shared personal experiences of being racially profiled and otherwise harassed by law enforcement officials. However, on most days there was no statistically significant difference in the participation rates of minority and nonminority students.

Despite the lack of empirical and observational studies of the impact of race on classroom participation, student race in the college classroom has been a topic of considerable interest. Pitt and Packard's (2012) study of blog postings by students in two sociology courses found no significant differences in the number of blogs written that referenced class, gender, sexual orientation, or family by white and black students. However, they did find a difference in regard to posts about the intersections between race and social institutions, with white students referencing these intersections more frequently than black students. Pitt and Packard (2012) concluded that black students contributed in two major ways. First, they would frequently invoke media depictions of race during discussions. Second, and consistent with Howard, Zoeller, and Pratt (2006), black students would bring descriptions of personal experiences with (and emotional responses to) social phenomena. By bringing their experiences in society into the classroom, black students provided their white peers with exposure to real-life experiences that they may never share because of their race (Pitt and Packard 2012). In a study of students' course journal entries, Packard (2011) found that black students were more likely than whites to write in autobiographical ways connecting their lived experience to social theory, whereas the white students' journal entries were more likely to be abstract and reference larger social institutions instead of personal experience.

In a study of 16 courses at a large Midwestern university, Trujillo (1986) found some evidence to suggest that nonminority students were asked significantly more complex questions by their professors, were pushed more to improve their responses, and received a greater amount of time during the processor's response to their questions and comments in comparison to minority students. The clear implication is that the professors in this study had lower expectations of minority students, though it is not clear that this assumption was consciously held by faculty members.

In his review of the literature, White (2011) concludes that there is "some evidence" that minority students participate less often in class discussion and that their participation has less of an impact on their learning compared to their nonminority classmates. White hypothesizes that lack of participation could be the result of fears of "acting white"—showing disrespect for one's minority culture by adopting the norms and behaviors of the dominant white culture in the college classroom. White (2011) conducted a semester-long study following four minority freshmen students. He found that all four students demonstrated feelings of "academic and linguistic incompetence" and were concerned with being expected to speak for the entirety of their respective cultures. The students' primary explanation for their reluctance to participate in classroom discussion was a lack of familiarity with the discursive styles common in college (White 2011, 259). These four minority students failed to see that adopting a different form of communication for a particular context is an additive process that could add to their repertoire of available discourses (Ogbu and Wilson 1990). Instead, they viewed such a switch as abandoning their culture of origin and "acting white."

As with student gender, instructors need to pay careful attention to any developing patterns of participation by race. Do minority students seem more reluctant to speak than nonminority students? Are both groups of students receiving the same type and same number of follow-up questions from the instructor? Can strategies that allow students time to collect and organize their thoughts prior to speaking help to equalize participate by race? Can instructors take advantage of and affirm minority students' willingness to make personal application of course concepts in ways that allow nonminority students to learn from their minority-student peers? With careful consideration and planning, students can do most of the work in the classroom and simultaneously help one another learn.

International Students and Participation in Discussion

As is the case with the role of students' race in relation to participation in classroom discussion, there is relatively little empirical research on the impact of students' country and culture of origin. That is, do international students participate differently than native students in American and Western college classrooms? While there is plenty of anecdotal evidence and speculation on the matter, one of the few empirical studies was conducted at a small private college in Malaysia with internationally diverse students (Mustapha 2010). The researcher was interested in the question of whether students from different parts of the world displayed different patterns of participation. Mustapha (2010) conducted interviews with 120 students, 84 of whom were international students. He found that students from African nations tended to report higher levels of participation than did students from the Middle East or Asia. Mustapha (2010) hypothesized that this difference may be due to the African students' greater mastery of the English language. By contrast, students from China were the most reluctant to speak up in class, remaining silent until they were called upon by their instructor. Mustapha's (2010) findings, at least with regard to Asian international students, confirm anecdotal evidence and conjecture at American colleges and universities that international students from Asia generally tend to be more reluctant to speak up in class and sometimes view doing so as showing disrespect toward the instructor.

Tatar (2005) found that graduate students from Turkey reported unfamiliarity with discussion as a learning pedagogy as their educational backgrounds did not require or encourage it. As non-native-English speakers the Turkish students felt less confident in participating. In a first-person account, Bista (2011) also describes how lacking familiarity with discussion as a classroom pedagogy and being a non-native-English speaker undermined the confidence necessary for participation. Similarly, Nakane (2005) in a study of Japanese students at Australian universities found that the Japanese students used silence in response to a variety of circumstances. Depending on the context, their silence could be indicative of a lack of understanding of course material, a lack of familiarity with classroom discourse norms, reluctance to compete with peers for the opportunity to speak, or the result of a cultural background where silence is considered polite. Therefore, instructors must be careful not to automatically assume that international students' lack of participation is indicative of a lack of interest in the course. In fact, their silence may be due to a lack of confidence. As we saw in Chapter 2, there are steps an instructor can take to improve students' confidence and facilitate participation. The lack of participation by international students may also signal their respect for the instructor rather than a lack of interest. Overtly addressing the purposes of engagement through discussion with all students at the beginning of a course, making it clear that participation is another learning tool, may also help international students understand the new classroom norms they are encountering and encourage their participation.

While individual factors, such as student gender, age, race, and country of origin, may impact students' level of participation, there are also contextual factors at work that shape classroom discussion. Both individual characteristics and contextual factors are important to keep in mind when creating classrooms that utilize student participation in discussion to facilitate learning and develop thinking skills.

Contextual Factors Influencing Participation

Contextual factors impacting participation in the college classroom include class size, instructor gender, seating arrangements, disciplinary area, and course level. Each of these variables may influence the amount of discussion in class and the percentage of students participating.

Class Size

Class size, meaning the number of students enrolled in a given course, is a variable that immediately comes to mind when we consider the contextual factors that are likely to influence students' participation in class. Based on personal experience most instructors will report that it is easier to get students to participate in smaller classes than in larger ones. However, as previously noted, the consolidation of responsibility tends to operate regardless of class size. A handful of students will do the vast majority of speaking in any class unless the instructor makes intentional efforts to change the norm. While research has demonstrated the consolidation of responsibility is in operation, class size has not always proven to have a statistically significant impact on students' participation.

In our (Howard, Zoeller, and Pratt's 2006) study of introductory sociology courses, the percentage of students participating in the one mass class (with an enrollment of 182 students) included in the sample of courses studied was about half of that in smaller sections (with a maximum enrollment of 45 students), despite quite successful efforts by the instructor in the mass class to make whole-class discussion a key pedagogy. In another observational study, we (Howard and Henney 1998) found that class size was negatively correlated with the amount of participation. However, in a third observational study we (Howard, James, and Taylor 2002) failed to find a statistically significant relationship between class size and the amount of participation in a course. It may be that the relationship between the number of students enrolled and overall amount of participation is not a linear relationship but one where class size can hit a significant *tipping point* where the size of the class discourages student participation. Nunn (1996), based on observations of courses with enrollments ranging from 15 to 44 students, did not find a strong relationship between class size and participation. However, Nunn (1996) did find that in classes with 35 or more students the percentage of time dedicated to discussion and the percentage of students participating in discussion fell off markedly, which supports the "tipping point" hypothesis.

Studies utilizing students' self-reports of participation have also generally pointed to a negative relationship between class size and participation. Crombie et al. (2003) found a small but significant effect of class size. Students in Auster and MacRone's (1994) study and the nursing students in Loftin, Davis, and Hartin's (2010) study reported that they were less likely to participate in larger classes than in smaller ones. Of course, one of the challenges in interpreting the impact of class size is what constitutes a large class. Students who attend large universities where some introductory courses may enroll hundreds of students might define a class of 40 as a "small" class, whereas students at a liberal arts college where the average class size is 15 may define a class of 25 as a "large" class. This complicates the relationship between class size and student participation. Students' perceptions of class size are likely more important than the number of students actually enrolled in a course. We will return to the topic of students' perceptions of the classroom and their responsibilities in the next chapter.

Instructor Gender

Instructor gender is another often-studied contextual factor regarding students' participation in discussion in the college classroom. While the findings are not as consistent as, say, the impact of student age, the preponderance of evidence suggests that having a female faculty member increases students' participation. As noted in my earlier caution, students are not likely to be consciously aware of the impact of instructor gender and are unlikely to self-report that instructor gender influences their participation. However, observations of students' interactions often suggest that instructor gender is a relevant contextual factor.

In an early study, Pearson and West (1991) found that male instructors received more questions from students than did female instructors. Other studies (Crombie et al. 2003; Howard and Henney 1998) found no significant difference in students' participation based on instructor gender. Yet multiple studies, particularly those utilizing observation as a methodology, have found an impact. Howard and Baird (2000) found significantly higher levels of participation in courses taught by female instructors compared to male instructors. Female instructors were significantly more likely to initiate interactions with students than were male instructors, though there was no significant difference in student-initiated interactions or interactions resulting from questions directed at particular students. Canada and Pringle (1995) found that female instructors initiated many more interactions in mixed-sex classes (though not in female-only classes). Howard, James, and Taylor (2002) also found that courses with female instructors had significantly higher rates of student participation. Howard, Zoeller, and Pratt (2006) found the percentage of students participating in courses with female instructors was almost twice that of courses with male instructors.

As Auster and MacRone (1994) astutely pointed out, this impact is not so much due to the faculty member's gender per se, but to the pedagogical strategies employed by the faculty member in the attempt to engage students in interaction. Female faculty members may be less likely than male faculty to rely on lecture as their sole or primary pedagogical strategy. That is, they are less likely to adopt the "sage on the stage" model of education. The pedagogical choices made by female faculty can have significant positive benefits for female students in particular. Based on students' self-reports, Fassinger (1995) found that female students were significantly more confident, comprehended more, were more interested in the subject matter, and participated more in classes when their professors were female. However, based on what we know about the benefits of participation for learning and the development of critical thinking skills, both male and female students are likely to benefit from the more interactive teaching styles of female faculty members.

Seating Arrangements, Disciplinary Area, and Course Level

Several other contextual factors have been investigated occasionally. Seating arrangement is one of them. Howard, Zoeller, and Pratt (2006) found that dominant talkers were disproportionally seated in the front-third of the room. Students in Loftin, Davis, and Hartin's (2010) study reported that if students were seated in a manner, such as a circle, that allowed them to see peers' quizzical or perplexed expressions, it encouraged students to speak up when they needed clarification.

Another contextual factor is the disciplinary area of the course. The impact of the course discipline is difficult to separate from instructor characteristics because the number of courses in any disciplinary area included in a particular research study is quite limited; thus the pedagogical approaches of a single or a few instructors can create differences that may or may not be related to disciplinary areas. The limitations due to small sample size included in observational studies lead to a greater reliance on student self-reports instead of classroom observation when attempting to assess the influence of disciplinary area. One study (Crombie et al. 2003) found that students reported greater participation in the arts and social sciences in comparison to courses in the natural sciences. In an early study, Barnes (1983) reported that the great majority of questions asked by college professors were at the lowest cognitive level—memory-oriented questions. Faculty in science, math, and engineering courses asked significantly more of these lower-level questions than did faculty in the humanities, social sciences, and arts. However, Barnes (1983) did not find any significant differences by disciplinary area in the number of higher-order questions asked.

The same difficulties are found when examining the impact of course level on student participation. One easily assumes that in smaller, more specialized upper-level courses the amount of inter-action would be greater. Yet the typically small number of courses included in observational studies makes it difficult to show a statis-tically significant difference (see, for example, Howard and Baird 2000). And once again, there is the issue of conflating the impact of individual instructors' pedagogical decisions with the impact of the level of the course. Despite these methodological constraints, Fritschner (2000) did find evidence that faculty members initiated more interactions in upper-level courses. Barnes (1983) failed to find any significant difference in the questioning levels used by pro-fessors in beginning and advanced-level courses and noted being surprised by the similarity of questions across course levels.

Summarizing the Research on Individual and Contextual Factors

To summarize with regard to individual factors we can draw some at least tentative conclusions. Nontraditional students are much more likely to speak up in class than traditionally aged (18- to 24-year-old) students. Student gender does not have a consistent impact in terms of either males or females participating more frequently. The impact of student race has not been sufficiently studied; while there is no consistently demonstrated finding regarding race, there are occasions when minority students will become the dominant talkers in class. International students, who are not native English speakers, are less likely to speak up in class. Regarding contextual factors, generally speaking, female instructors are doing a better job of engaging students in discussion than male instructors. This may well have more to do with a greater willingness on the part of the female instructors to utilize pedagogical strategies that engage students than with instructor gender directly. Increasing class size does reduce at least some students' willingness to participate in discussion, but perceptions of what constitutes a large class will vary by the particular institutional context. Other factors, such as seating arrangements, disciplinary area, and course level, have been shown to sometimes impact the level of participation.

The Love–Hate Relationship between Talkers and Non-talkers

Having utilized the research findings to identify the students most likely to accept the consolidation of responsibility and those most likely to avoid participating in discussion, what do these two groups of students think of one another? What do the non-talkers think of talkers and vice versa?

The quieter students in your courses likely have a love–hate relationship with the dominant talkers. On the one hand, non-talkers are grateful that the talkers assume responsibility for speaking up when the instructor expects it. After all, this relieves the non-talkers of that burden. Yet, the relationship is sometimes strained. In our (Howard, Short, and Clark 1996) interviews, 22 students from the observed courses made a nearly equal number of positive comments and negative comments about the dominant talkers in their classes. These students showed appreciation for their talkative peers for asking questions and clarifying issues for them. In another study utilizing student interviews, we (Howard and Baird 2000) also found that the non-talkers were particularly appreciative when talkers asked for clarification on points of confusion.

However, non-talkers expressed frustration when they perceived that talkers were talking too frequently, spending too much time sharing personal anecdotes, belaboring a topic longer than peers perceived to be appropriate, or preventing classmates from hearing from the person they defined as the true expert—the instructor (see Howard and Baird 2000; Howard, Short, and Clark 1996). Another way talkers sometimes annoyed their less-talkative classmates had to do with the timing of their comments (Howard, Short, and Clark 1996). Occasionally it was clear that the instructor had finished a few minutes before the official end-time for class. Typically the instructor would then ask, "Are there any questions?" The last thing most non-talkers wanted at that moment was for a talker to ask a question or make a comment that prolonged class instead of allowing students to be dismissed early.

In our analysis of students' self-reports, we (Howard, Short, and Clark 1996) found that students were more likely to get annoyed with other students who "talk too much" than to get annoyed with students who "do not participate in class discussion." Yet for the instructors in these same courses, the opposite was true. Instructors were more likely to be annoyed with the nonparticipating students than with the dominant talkers. If a student was doing well in the course otherwise, instructors would presume the quiet student was simply shy. However, if the student was not doing well otherwise, they tended to assume that the student either was not showing appropriate interest in the course or had not completed the reading assignment. So while talkers risk being seen in a negative light by their classmates, non-talkers risk instructors making negative assumptions in response to their silence.

While instructors tend to have a more positive view of dominant talkers than do students, there is still something of a love–hate relationship between instructors and talkers as well. When a talker talks too much, takes the class off topic, or seems to have a compulsive need to speak without having anything substantive to contribute, instructors can also become annoyed with talkers. So the challenge of managing effective classroom discussion includes increasing the percentage of students participating and ensuring that dominant talkers neither sidetrack discussions nor become the objects of classmates' scorn.

Improving Discussion through Course Design

Awareness is the first step in changing the patterns identified in the research. As an instructor I should be constantly asking myself, Who is talking in my classroom? Are certain categories of students dominating the discussions while others silently observe? Can I change any of the contextual factors such as seating arrangement or class size in hopes of increasing student participation? If I cannot change seating arrangement or enrollment caps, can I engage in active learning and small-group strategies that will make my large class seem smaller? Can I increase the number of questions I ask? Can I change from more superficial memory/recall-level questions to questions that require higher-order thinking skills such as synthesis and analysis? As I seek to change my students' behavior in the classroom, I need to remember that I may well have to change my own behavior in the classroom as I try to ensure that it is the students who are doing the most work and therefore the most learning.

Just as there are pedagogical strategies that can help overcome the norm of civil attention in the college classroom, instructors can adopt approaches (including many of the same ones) that can reduce the impact of the consolidation of responsibility. Fassinger (1995) insightfully argues that an instructor's greatest impact is the result of course design decisions. By creating a course that includes activities that require student-to-student as well as student-to-instructor interaction in a supportive emotional climate, faculty members can greatly increase both the percentage of students participating in discussion and total amount of discussion occurring. Therefore, Fassinger (1995) recommends starting the semester with discussions and exercises that communicate to students that their participation is an expectation in the course.

As noted in Chapter 2, the first day of class is very important for establishing a new norm in class. If students, females or males, have experienced a chilly climate with regard to participation, been made to feel as if their comments were unwelcome, or that they were missing something that "should be obvious" when they asked a question, they will quickly conclude that the instructor does not want student participation. Students look for clues regarding the desirability of discussion in a course and will quickly shut down if they perceive that a student who speaks up in class has been mistreated by the professor or peers (Loftin, Davis, and Hartin 2010). If it becomes clear in the first couple of class periods that having only a few students speaking up in class will satisfy the instructor, then the norm of the consolidation of responsibility will take hold firmly. Therefore it is important to create a classroom environment that feels safe for all students and, equally important, to find ways to slow down the dominant talkers, allowing other students the opportunity to participate without making anyone feel as if their input is unwelcome.

Slowing Down the Dominant Talkers by Limiting Who Can Respond

One very simple way to increase the percentage of students participating in discussion is to limit who can respond to a particular question. For example, you might say, "Let's hear from someone who hasn't spoken up today." Or "I've heard a lot from the men in class today. What do women think about this topic?" Or "Those sitting in the front of the room have had a lot to say. What about those of you sitting in the back half of the room?" You can also do this by walking to a different location in the classroom and saying, "I haven't heard any comments from those of you over here. I'd be interested in hearing what you think." It is always a good idea to preface your limitation on who can speak, by first affirming those you are going to exclude from responding. For example, you could say, "We've had some really great input so far, but I want to hear from someone who hasn't spoken up yet." Or "The gals have had some great insights on this topic. Come on, guys, what do you think?" In this manner, you are both expressing your appreciation for the dominant talkers who speak without much prompting from you and simultaneously limiting their participation while you invite the more quiet students to join in the discussion.

Slowing Down the Dominant Talkers by Inviting Others to Respond

Another approach is to limit your own talking. Instead of you responding to a dominant talker's comment or question, ask other students to respond. For example, in a nursing class, one could say, "Kevin is asking a really good question here: How does a nurse interject what is important but perhaps overlooked information regarding a patient without offending the doctor? Who has a suggestion for Kevin?" The danger, of course, is that another of the dominant talkers may be the one who volunteers to respond. In those cases you may again need to limit who can respond. Or you may first allow another dominant talker to offer a response, providing the more introverted students time to reflect and gather their thoughts, then limit who can respond in hopes of drawing more students into the conversation.

While slowing down the dominant talkers is one side of the equation that leads to more equitable classroom discussion, increasing the participation of quieter, particularly younger students, is the other.

Encouraging Quiet Students: The One Minute Paper

Whenever you want to increase the percentage of students participating in discussion, it's always a good idea to allow students time to collect their thoughts before asking them to speak up in class. The One Minute Paper is a simple technique for doing so (Angelo and Cross 1993, 148). The instructor simply asks a question and allows students 60 seconds to write in response to it. Writing the question on the board or on a PowerPoint slide is helpful. This strategy is beneficial for more introverted students who are less likely to speak up until they have had the opportunity to decide just what it is they think about the question. This approach also can help with

dominant talkers who may have a tendency to ramble alou
determine what they think about the question. By forcing th.
to write before speaking, you are more likely to get a well-focused
response from the dominant talkers.

Encouraging Quiet Students: The Muddiest Point

The Muddiest Point is a variation of the One Minute Paper, which
can be utilized at the conclusion of class period (Angelo and Cross
1993, 154). Two or three minutes prior to the end of the class
session, the instructor asks students to take out a sheet of paper and
write about one thing they did not clearly understand from that
day's class. What topic was most difficult to understand? What did
they seem to "not get"? Students hand in their responses on the way
out of class. The instructor then reviews the feedback and begins
the following class session addressing the most common topics
brought up in the Muddiest Point papers. While the Muddiest
Point papers are often anonymous, instructors can require students
to include their names as a means of taking attendance or to use as
a springboard to launching discussion in the following class period.
You could begin the class by saying, "Megan and Jamal both point
out that I didn't do a very good job of explaining the difference
between inductive and deductive reasoning last class period. And
I'm willing to bet they are not the only ones I left confused. How
many would like to have the difference explained again? Would
anyone like to take a crack at it and see if you can do a better job
than I did?" Then, once a classmate or two has responded, you
can ask Megan and Jamal, "Does that make sense? How would you
summarize the distinction now that we've had a few other attempts
to explain it?"

Note that it helps create a safe environment for participation if
you, as the instructor, take ownership of the problem. Your default
position is that you didn't do a good enough job of making the point
clear. You also invite greater participation by asking classmates to
play the role of expert, or at least the role of ally, in attempting

to clarify. And you have the opportunity to ask Megan and Jamal to join in the discussion by summarizing and reinforcing the distinction after classmates have come to their aid. This approach reinforces the notion that learning is a community endeavor. Students can learn from one another as well as from the instructor. By noting your own weakness or shortcomings as an instructor, you are also creating a less threatening (less chilly) climate for all students. If the instructor can admit that he doesn't know everything or needs help in making things clear, it's certainly okay for students to do the same.

Encouraging Quiet Students: The Most Important Point

Another classroom assessment technique that can be used at the end of a class period and perhaps in conjunction with the Muddiest Point (Angelo and Cross 1993, 154) is the Most Important Point. In the last few minutes of class, ask students to take out a sheet of paper and write down the most important point made in class that day. It could be something the instructor said or it could be something a classmate said. This strategy encourages students to stop and reflect on their learning. What have we learned today? Why is it important? The instructor then reviews these prior to the following class period. At the start of the next class, she can affirm students for identifying key points as a quick review and warmup for the day's topic. Rather than you as the instructor summarizing the key points, you can also pass back papers as students enter the classroom and then call upon students who do not routinely volunteer to participate in discussion. "Jacob, you hit upon a key topic in your paper. Would you please share it with your classmates and tell us why you thought it was the most important point?" "Arielle, your paper also captured some key ideas. Tell us what you wrote and why you felt it was most important."

If students have overlooked what you felt was the most important point of the previous class, this is a second chance to reiterate it. Again, it is good for you as the instructor to take ownership of any confusion by saying things like, "While you (the students) noted numerous important points from last class session, no one (or only a few) mentioned the importance of World War II for lifting the United States out of the lingering effects of the Great Depression. I must have rushed through that part of the lecture. Let me summarize that point again because it is important for understanding this topic." Better still, call upon the one or two students who hit the Most Important Point to reiterate why they chose it as the most important point of the day.

The Most Important Point can be used in conjunction with the Muddiest Point. If students feel that everything was clear, instead of writing "Everything was clear," they have to reflect upon the class from a somewhat different angle, "What was most important?" So by combing the two strategies you allow students a choice of which to address as they reflect upon their learning in the class session. In either case, as the instructor you can utilize these student reflections as a way of inviting less-talkative students into the conversation while affirming their insights prior to their having to speak up in front of classmates.

Creating a Safe Environment for Non-native Speakers

In order to encourage the participation of non-native speakers, it's not only important to provide time to think before speaking, it's also helpful to provide opportunities to rehearse their comments in a smaller group before addressing the larger class. (This is true not only for non-native speakers, but for all students.) The classroom assessment technique Think-Pair-Share (Angelo and Cross 1993), described in detail in Chapter 2, is one way to do this. By giving non-native speakers an opportunity to share their thoughts with one classmate first, they will be more likely to share with the class as a whole. Even if the students don't share with the class as a whole, they will be engaged by sharing their thinking with a classmate and will have had the opportunity to practice their language skills in class.

The practice need not be limited to pairs. Students can be arranged in small groups of three to five for discussion of a topic or a question. Each student can have 30 seconds or one minute to share their thoughts without interruption from group members. After everyone has spoken, the group has an additional one to two minutes to summarize their thinking collectively and report back to the class.

A third method for inviting the input of non-native speakers is to provide an opportunity to contribute to the discussion in an online forum. Utilizing discussion in an online format will be the topic of Chapter 5. But for now let me point out the advantages of online discussion for non-native speakers. Online forums allow students to write and share their thoughts rather than having to speak them in front of other students. This exercise gives students the time to reflect, write, and correct prior to sharing. Online discussion forums can be one effective means of getting shy or introverted students to share their insights and questions. Most instructors have had the experience of the best student in the course being one who never speaks up during class. An online discussion forum is one way to pull them into the conversation so that their peers can benefit from their insights. All of this certainly applies to non-native speakers as well. Allowing them the opportunity to reflect, write, and correct prior to sharing their thoughts makes their participation much safer.

Something to keep in mind when teaching non-native speakers (who may come from different cultural backgrounds) as well as members of minority groups is to avoid asking them to speak for everyone in their demographic category. Just as we don't expect one white student to speak for all whites, or one male student to speak for all males, we should be careful to avoid placing that burden on minority or international students. However, you can bring the online discussion into the classroom in order to increase the participation of quieter students. Review the online discussion forums prior to class. When you note that a quiet student, a non-native-English speaker, or a minority student makes a particularly salient point, you can call on them by name to repeat their insight during class. For example, you could say, "Tameka, you made a really important point in the online forum yesterday. Would you be willing to repeat what you said for the benefit of those who may have been skimming through the forum too quickly?" By affirming Tameka before asking her to speak up in class, you let her know that she has something important to contribute and that it is safe to do so. This helps to create a welcoming environment for students who may be reluctant to volunteer to participate.

Making Larger Classes Feel Smaller

Perhaps the most obvious thing one can do to make any class feel smaller is change the arrangement of the furniture so that students can see one another's faces. This might mean arranging the tablet armchairs into a circle or arranging the tables into a large rectangle or horseshoe arrangement. As we noted before, when students can see one another's puzzled looks they are more likely to ask for clarification when needed. Even in a class that utilizes lecture frequently, placing seats in a horseshoe arrangement that allows students both to see the instructor at the front and to see many of their classmates' faces can make the classroom feel smaller. If you do rearrange furniture in your classrooms, it's important to ask students to help you return it to the institution's prescribed arrangement at the end of class in order to avoid tensions with other faculty members who teach in the same room. A little bit of courtesy toward your colleagues can go a long way in avoiding conflict.

However, sometimes the physical environment of the classroom is fixed. Tables are in neat rows facing the front of the room and bolted to the floor. Or you are in a theater-style classroom with fixed seats facing a stage in the front of the room. While such arrangements are less conducive to making the classroom feel smaller, you can still utilize pedagogical strategies like Think-Pair-Share or small groups to create a welcoming environment. You can ask students in row one to turn around and form a group with students in row two. And ask students in row three to partner with those in row four and so on.

Another option is to assign students in large classes to semester-long small groups of six to eight. On the first day of class students spend a few minutes introducing themselves to their fellow group members and exchanging contact information. That way, should a student miss class, she has someone she can call upon to get notes or a summary of the day's activities. These small groups are then the building blocks for class discussion. Students can be required to sit with the other members of their groups. Then, rather than calling for large-group discussion, ask each group to quickly discuss the topic or respond to the question. The instructor can then ask a few of the groups to quickly report back to the class as a whole.

The key in large classes is to repeatedly break the large class into smaller components—pairs or small groups. While some students will never feel comfortable speaking out in a whole-class discussion, when you utilize small groups students will feel as if they have a few peers with whom they are comfortable interacting and they may feel that they are not entirely anonymous in class despite the large size.

Instructor Gender, Discipline, and Course Level

Instructor gender, disciplinary area, and course level are three contextual factors influencing student participation in discussion that are not changeable. But they are not inherently limiting factors, either. Male instructors can adopt the interactive, collaborative pedagogies more frequently utilized by female faculty members. Science instructors can utilize the same pedagogies as faculty in the humanities and the social sciences. I had a colleague in Chemistry who utilized frequent writing assignments as pedagogical tools. When students would complain about the unusual amount of writing in a science class, his standard reply was, "Every class is a writing class!" He was firmly convinced that writing was a pedagogical tool that helped students learn chemistry more effectively, so there was every reason to adopt a strategy more frequently associated with humanities courses. The same is true of course level. Lower-level courses in your discipline may traditionally be taught in a lecture-heavy format that doesn't allow for much interaction with students, but they don't have to be. Even in large introductory course sections, an instructor can adopt strategies to make large classes feel smaller—strategies that are more typically utilized in upper-level courses primarily populated by majors.

Conclusion

As we saw in Chapter 2 with our discussion of the norm of civil attention, changing a college classroom norm takes intentional effort on the part of the instructor. The same is true with the norm of the consolidation of responsibility. It is easy to believe that we have done a wonderful job of involving students in discussion, but a closer examination can reveal that what we really did was a wonderful job of involving a handful of students while the vast majority of students were simply spectators. This is another default norm in the college classroom unless we choose to make it otherwise. There are a wide variety of pedagogical strategies available to instructors to both increase the amount of discussion occurring in class and increase the percentage of students participating in discussion.

We have now identified two key college classroom norms pertaining to discussion and considered how to change them. But underlying these different norms are students' diverse understandings of what could and should be happening in the classroom and what in particular is fair to expect of them. This is the topic of Chapter 4.

4

Students' Differing Definitions
of the Classroom

It's that day again—the one when last semester's course evaluations arrive. As you hold the envelope in your hands, your
stomach churns. You do your best to help students learn. Last
semester you even took some risks and sought to engage students
more frequently in discussion. Will students appreciate your efforts
or will they punish you for using new approaches that weren't
well polished? What will your department chair have to say? Will
he once again want to discuss every negative comment? At the
end of the semester, you felt pretty good about the class. It could
have been better, of course, but most days students did participate
in wide-ranging discussions. Your palms are sweaty as you skip
past the quantitative scores and head straight to the students'
comments.

You are struck almost immediately by how the comments
contradict each other. The first expresses appreciation of the
discussions while the next complains that too much time was
wasted on listening to others who don't have your expertise. One
student writes, "The discussions in class really helped me learn
the content." Shortly after, you read this comment: "I didn't know
what I should be getting out of the discussions. They seemed point-
less and unrelated to what was on the exams." Several students
clearly resent the fact that you made participation in discussion a
requirement while others note that doing so helped them improve
their course grade. What's an instructor supposed to make of such

contradictory feedback? You keep hearing about how engaging students increases learning. But it appears a sizeable number of students resent your attempts to increase their participation. Why the inconsistent response? Why do some students seem to appreciate your efforts to stop being the "sage on the stage" while that's exactly what others want you to be? Feedback like this can drive a faculty member crazy.

Students' Definitions of the College Classroom

Sociologists note that social contexts must be defined (Berger and Luckmann 1967). How participants in an interaction define a situation will determine what behaviors they see as appropriate for that context (Goffman 1959; McHugh 1968). The college classroom is no exception. Students' satisfaction with a course and their willingness to engage in certain activities will depend in part on how well the instructor's definition of what is and ought to be happening in the classroom aligns with their own. An important part of the process is defining the roles, the expectations for behavior, of both the instructor and students.

Recall that these definitions and role expectations are not developed from scratch. We bring years of experience in similar contexts to our interactions. The normative social expectations we have learned in the past will influence our initial assumptions about what is going on in a particular situation. Recall the elevator norms discussed in Chapter 1. When we ride a particular elevator for the first time, we do not reinvent the wheel. We rely on our past experiences, which have taught us what is and is not appropriate behavior for riding on an elevator. We face the front. We divide up the space to allow one another as much personal space as possible. We limit interaction with strangers to a smile, a nod of the head, or small-talk. We don't have to wonder each time we step onto a new elevator—is this one of those where we face the front? Or will other passengers expect me to face the rear or the side of the elevator instead? Elevator norms are nearly universal. We don't spend any time or energy wondering about which direction we should face when we step on board a particular elevator for the first time.

The college classroom has clear normative expectations as well. In Chapter 2, we explored the norm of civil attention. In Chapter 3, we described the individual and contextual factors that help to determine which students are most likely to be the dominant talkers who accept the consolidation of responsibility for participation and which students are most likely to be only occasional contributors to class discussion. Fortunately for instructors who want to engage their students in the pursuit of greater learning, there is enough variation in how college courses are structured to allow instructors, as well as students, some room for negotiation in the definition of the situation in the classroom. Students have encountered some courses where the only person who ever talks in class is the instructor. They likely have also been in courses that were very interactive with high expectations for student participation. Students may have experienced courses with a significant amount of peer-to-peer collaborative learning. So there is a continuum of experiences with college courses from the expectation for high levels of student engagement to the expectation that students will be very passive. But the majority of students' experiences in higher education are likely to have had a heavy focus on the faculty member with an expectation for some participation, at least on the part of a few students. In sum, students will assume that civil attention and the consolidation of responsibility are the operative norms unless faculty members make intentional efforts to communicate a different set of norms and a new definition of the situation. Without those intentional efforts to help students redefine their understandings of the classroom, they may resent, or even actively resist, changes and are likely to express their frustrations in the end-of-semester course evaluations.

Therefore it's important to know our starting point. How do students define their own and the instructor's responsibilities in class? What reasons do they give for their own participation or lack of participation? With an understanding of how students define the college classroom and what they think is expected of them, we can then begin the process of creating a new definition and new expectations.

Students' Views of Their Responsibilities in College Courses

What do students typically see as their responsibilities in the college classroom? Through a series of studies, my colleagues and I have found high levels of agreement that students perceive they should complete assigned tasks, attend class, study, learn the material, pay attention in class, and ask for help when needed (Howard and Baird 2000; Howard, James, and Taylor 2002; Howard, Zoeller, and Pratt 2006). However, there was one area of consistent and significant disagreement between students who are dominant talkers and students who are less frequent participants in class. Given the topic of this book, you can guess what that difference is. Talkers are significantly more likely than non-talkers to agree that students are responsible for participation in class discussion (Howard and Baird 2000; Howard, James, and Taylor 2002).

This difference in how talkers and non-talkers define their classroom responsibilities has been shown in a variety of contexts. First Year Seminar students studied by Goodman, Murphy, and D'Andrea (2012) did not perceive that verbal participation was required of them, viewing discussion as strictly voluntary. Fritschner (2000) found that the quieter students defined participation much more broadly than did talkative students. For quieter students, participation included things like attendance, paying attention, active listening, and doing homework. So in their view, they could be actively "participating" in class without ever speaking—a point of view the instructor may not share.

Interestingly, Goodman, Murphy, and D'Andrea (2012) also found that the creation of a safe, supportive classroom environment, at least when not combined with explicit expectations for participation, can potentially undermine an instructor's efforts to engage students in discussion. In their study, students' desire to be supportive of each other (part of a safe environment) didn't allow for them to express disagreement. Therefore, the professor's emphasis on a supportive, encouraging environment caused students to perceive it was acceptable to not participate and absolutely inappropriate to challenge a classmate's statements. After all, a supportive environment can be easily construed to be a situation wherein one is never made uncomfortable or asked to do anything he or she would rather not do. As they explored students' emotional reactions to and understandings of the classroom, Goodman, Murphy, and D'Andrea (2012) also found a tension between students' beliefs that they ideally should be both invested in classroom discussions and emotionally detached. Given this tension, some students chose to not speak when they were the most emotionally invested or held the strongest beliefs about the topic. This may have been a strategy to prevent students' sense of self or core beliefs from being subject to uncomfortable scrutiny. However, as instructors we need to be careful not to make assumptions that reflect poorly upon students' decision not to participate verbally.

Reda (2009) conducted a yearlong study of a first-year composition course in which students were occasionally asked to write about their experience of classroom silence. Through class members' writing and through interviews with five of the students, Reda (2009) concluded that students tended to perceive speaking in class to be a high-stakes situation amounting to an oral exam in which they were expected to provide the "right" answer. If the instructor graded participation, the stakes were even higher for students. Reda (2009) found that students, through their observations of the instructor, would assess the types of questions asked and the instructor's responses to student input to determine if they were being asked to reflect, speculate, hypothesize, or perform on what they considered to be an oral quiz. Reda's (2009) students, like those of Goodman, Murphy, and D'Andrea (2012), were also quite concerned with their classmates' perceptions and how perceptions of the speaker could be shaped by what a student says in class. This situation made it risky for students to verbally disagree with or challenge the views of their classmates. For example, Reda (2009) noted that challenging a peer on a highly charged topic like affirmative action could result in being branded a racist. Therefore, not only was participation viewed as stressful because it was perceived as an oral quiz, it was also hazardous in that it could result in classmates developing unfavorable views of you.

While faculty members often think that controversial topics are great for discussion, students may not see them that way. Whether one is discussing evolution, global warming, gun control, abortion, or any liberal-versus-conservative topic, the faculty member may see these as interesting topics for students to debate and discuss. However, our students may perceive them as quite threatening to their sense of self or to dearly held beliefs and as dangerous topics because of the risk of classmates' negative judgments of them.

One strategy for helping students discuss such sensitive and strongly held topics is to ask them to articulate the opposite perspective of the one they personally hold. You can justify this by suggesting that in order to defend one's position you must understand your critic's position. If you held a pro–gun control perspective, what arguments could you make against gun control? If students are attempting to place themselves in the role of another who thinks differently than they do, they are learning to view a topic, such as gun control, from a different perspective. In so doing they learn both the strengths and weaknesses of their dearly held positions.

Each of the studies cited above points to the complexities of defining the situation in the college classroom, particularly when it comes to participation. What the instructor may see as a collaborative construction of knowledge, students may perceive as a high-stakes test made even more dangerous because of the risk of a negative social judgment by one's peers. These findings point to a need for instructors to involve students in a discussion about discussion by making explicit our understandings and expectations for discussion (e.g., "Not only are you not expected to always provide the 'right' answer, in many cases there is no single right answer"). Additionally, there is a need to vary the format of discussion from whole-class discussion to small groups to pairs to online forums in order to reduce the sense of risk involved for students. Later in this chapter we identify some strategies to assist with this goal.

Students' Views of Faculty Responsibilities in College Courses

Not only do students attempt to identify and understand their own roles as they develop their definition of the situation in your classroom, they are attempting to explicate the role and expectations of the instructor. As noted before, students attempt to assess the type of input the instructor may be seeking in classroom discussion (Reda 2009). They also try to determine whether the instructor desires their participation at all. And what students perceive about expectations for discussion may be different from what the instructor thinks he or she is communicating. For example, in one study I conducted with colleagues, we (Howard, Short, and Clark 1996) found that instructors perceived themselves pausing for and inviting students to participate in discussion more frequently than did their students. The instructors included in the study felt they were offering frequent and safe invitations for participation, while students felt instructors moved on quickly without allowing sufficient time for students to first contemplate and then respond.

Different groups of students may interpret the instructor's behaviors in the classroom in a dissimilar fashion. Students identified as talkers, who accepted the consolidation of responsibility for student participation, in Howard and Baird's (2000) study were significantly more likely to agree that the instructor paused long enough and frequently enough to allow for student questions and comments than were quieter students. Crombie et al. (2003) found that active participators regarded their professors as more positive, as more personalizing, and as stimulating more discussion than did other students in the same class who perceived themselves as less active participators. In addition, the active participators had a more positive impression of their professors overall compared to the less active students (Crombie et al. 2003), which certainly has the potential to influence their ratings and comments on end-of-semester course evaluations.

In terms of their expectations of the instructor role, talkers and non-talkers tend to agree that the instructor should be knowledge-able, make class interesting, follow the syllabus, motivate students to participate in discussion, and know students by name (Howard and Baird 2000). However, talkers were significantly more likely to say that instructors should help them "think critically about material" than were non-talkers (Howard and Baird 2000). This may reflect a difference in preparedness between talkers and non-talkers for what Roberts (2002) calls *deep learning*—a topic to which we return later in this chapter. Howard, James, and Taylor (2002) found that talkers differed from non-talkers in their expectations on a number of levels. Talkers were significantly more likely to agree that it is part of the instructor's responsibility to know students' names, to motivate students, to encourage discussion, and to pause long enough and often enough to allow students to participate.

Students' expectation that the instructor be knowledgeable about the subject matter can be something of a double-edged sword. When students view the faculty member as the sole source of authoritative knowledge, it can reduce students' self-confidence, increase their fear of criticism, and thereby hinder participation (Weaver and Qi 2005). Given that self-confidence is a strong predictor of student participation, anything that undermines students' self-confidence will inhibit discussion. So while students rightfully expect the instructor to be knowledgeable, instructors must be careful not to create a definition of the situation wherein the instructor is the only source of knowledge and understanding. When an instructor over-relies on lecture, it is easy for students to perceive her as the only authoritative source of knowledge in the class. By taking intentional steps to involve students actively in class, we can make them co-creators of knowledge and understanding. Finding the proper balance between a focus on the instructor, who does (hopefully) bring added value to the class through her training and expertise, and engaging students in each other's teaching and learning is a challenge. The proper balance will likely vary based on the subject matter of the course, the course level, and the instructor's pedagogical strengths and weaknesses. Goodman, Murphy, and D'Andrea (2012) note that students may themselves split over whether the instructor should focus on covering the material or having student-centered discussions with some seeing discussion as desirable while others prefer the instructor-centered focus on the material.

Why Students Choose to Participate

Given that talkers and non-talkers often define the classroom in a somewhat different manner, what reasons do they give for their own participation or lack of participation in discussion? As noted earlier, student confidence is an important predictor of participation (Weaver and Qi 2005). When students feel confident and safe in the classroom, they are more likely to verbally participate for a variety of reasons. As would be expected, talkers often tend to be significantly more likely than non-talkers to cite a variety of reasons as motivating their participation.

In one study we (Howard and Henney 1998) found that talkers were significantly more likely than non-talkers to say they participated because they were "seeking information or clarification," they "have something to contribute," and they "learn by participating." Two of students' top three reasons given for participation in discussion in both Howard and Baird (2000) and

Howard, James, and Taylor (2002), "having something to share" and "learning more through participation," were cited significantly more frequently by talkers than non-talkers. There was not a significant difference between talkers and non-talkers on the third reason, "seeking clarification." Howard, Zoeller, and Pratt (2006) also found the top two reasons for students' participation were "having something to share" and "seeking clarification."

While a less commonly cited reason for participation, talkers were significantly more likely to say that they participated because "if they did not, no one else would" (Howard and Baird 2000). Talkers were also more likely to say they participate because "it makes class more interesting," because the "instructor creates comfortable atmosphere by talking about him- or herself," and because they "are familiar and comfortable with classmates" (Howard, James, and Taylor 2002).

These findings collectively point back to the issue of confidence. Talkers are more likely than non-talkers to believe that they have something worthwhile to contribute to the class. They see themselves as active participants in the construction of learning and understanding. Talkers are also more likely to believe the classroom is a safe environment and to be comfortable with their classmates, thus allowing them to have the necessary confidence for participation. So an issue instructors must address is how do we increase the confidence of non-talkers, helping them to understand that they, too, have something to contribute to their peers' learning?

How does an instructor do this? One key is certainly how you handle an incorrect or a not particularly good answer. It is absolutely important to affirm student input whenever you can; even when the response is not particularly good, you can say, "Jake has gotten us started with some general thoughts. Who can build upon Jake's starting point and help us go deeper?" It is easy to stop listening when we think a student is off-track. But every mistake a student makes is a window into their thinking. How and why did they get off-track? It is very likely that there are silent students in the room who made the same mistake or the same faulty assumptions. If we can understand a student's logic that led to a poor answer, we might find that our explanation skipped a step, something that we took for granted, but something that students needed to be made explicit. If an instructor can persuade students that "we are all in this together" and if students are not learning as well or as quickly as hoped, the instructor as well as the students may have some culpability. As an instructor, being willing to admit one's own shortcomings and imperfections in the classroom can help students feel safe enough to take the risks associated with participation.

Why Students Choose Not to Participate

Talkers tend to believe they have something to contribute to discussion. Through their actions they become active participants in the construction of knowledge and understanding. Non-talkers are much less confident in their ability to make a similar contribution. Sixsmith, Dyson, and Nataatmadja (2006) found that a majority of students in their study cited a lack of knowledge or understanding of the topic as a key reason for their lack of participation. This lack of confidence was accentuated by a lack of preparation for class. The students studied by Sixsmith, Dyson, and Nataatmadja (2006) also reported that perceiving a topic to be boring, shyness, language problems, and fears of speaking in front of the whole class or of "saying something stupid" were reasons for their nonparticipation.

Weaver and Qi (2005) reported much the same thing in their examination of the informal structure of the classroom. Students' fear of peer disapproval had a large negative effect on self-reported participation. Students' fears were influenced by their level of preparation as well. Students were fearful of having their lack of preparation exposed in front of the instructor and their peers and therefore chose not to participate in discussion.

Other studies have also pointed to students' lack of preparation as a reason for their nonparticipation. In a couple of my own studies, male students (Howard, Short, and Clark 1996) and traditional students (Howard and Henney 1998) cited a lack of preparation as reason for not participating in discussion significantly more often than female students and nontraditional students. Ironically, in another study we (Howard, Short, and Clark 1996) found that while males were more likely to admit they did not prepare for class, females were more likely to say they didn't know enough about the subject matter and that their ideas were not well enough formulated in order to participate. The large size of the class was also a factor in some students' lack of participation even when the average class size included in the studies was 15 (Howard, Short, and Clark 1996) or 20 (Howard, James, and Taylor 2002) students. This suggests that even when classes are relatively small, some, particularly females and traditional students, may perceive the class to be too large for safe participation.

Based on the research, we can have a reasonable idea of the default definition of the situation that students are likely to bring to the classroom. We know that many do not automatically assume that participation in class discussion is a part of their responsibility as students. We know that many students expect the instructor to be the sole authority in the classroom and this expectation can inhibit their participation. We know that talkers, more than non-talkers, are likely to believe that they have something to contribute to the class and to be willing to seek clarification when needed. We know that a lack of preparation will inhibit students' participation in class. And we know that even when a class may seem sufficiently small to the instructor, some students will define the class as too large for them to risk participation. So how is an instructor to respond to these definitions of the situation in the classroom?

Redefining the Classroom

Perhaps the first step an instructor can take to redefine the class-room in a way that will facilitate students' participation with the goal of increasing learning is to have a discussion about discussion.

This needs to happen on the first day of class and needs to be rein-forced in the syllabus. Sharing the learning objectives for the course and the strategies you as the instructor have adopted to help stu-dents achieve them can help students redefine the classroom situa-tion and their role within it.

Deep Structure Learning

Roberts (2002) argues that our learning objectives need to go well beyond the content to what he calls *deep structure learning*. By deep structure learning objectives, Roberts (2002) means those capac-ities and skills that are prerequisite to independent, creative, and critical thinking. The goal of an undergraduate education should be, therefore, to help students move from lower-order thinking skills, a concrete-operational mode of thought (e.g., there is always one "correct" answer), toward deeper levels of thinking. Roberts (2002) ties this goal to the social construction of the classroom. Freshmen students are often unfamiliar and uncomfortable with notions such as the existence of multiple legitimate perspectives and the lack of a single, straightforward correct answer. They must begin to grapple with this type of thinking if they are to develop their cognitive capacities. While some students will embrace this change in the approach to learning and in learning objectives, others will find it quite uncomfortable. Faculty and students' differing definitions of the classroom lead to a number of what Roberts (2002) calls "ironies of effective teaching."

As we seek to change students' definitions of the college class-room and their role in it, while simultaneously seeking to promote deep structure learning, we face a number of ironies or tensions (Roberts 2002). Several of these are relevant to how we increase students' participation and to what end. First, we must recognize that content matters. But if we focus only on content, we may fail to help our students develop the higher-order thinking skills that should be the goal of a college education regardless of the stu-dent's major. Instructors constantly face the question, How does one balance student participation that enhances learning with a concern for coverage of the material?

Second, what Roberts calls *benign disruption*, making students a bit uncomfortable by challenging their assumptions and preconceptions, is an effective pedagogical tool for developing high-order thinking, but it may undermine student–instructor rapport or make the classroom environment feel less safe and supportive for students. We have seen research again and again point to the importance of a safe environment for student participation.

Third, an instructor's effective role performance through careful organization of the course (an often-undervalued aspect of effective teaching) and energetic, enthusiastic presentation can engage students in learning, but at the same time might intimidate them into silence because of their perceived inability to replicate the instructor's polished performance. One step to overcoming these ironies of effective teaching is to address them head on through a discussion about discussion.

Having a Discussion about Discussion

Instructors often take it for granted that knowledge is socially constructed, that students can learn from their peers as well as their instructor, and being engaged with the material, classmates, and the instructor will facilitate both their learning of the material and the development of critical thinking skills. In their review of the early scholarship, Braxton, Eimers, and Bayer (1996) noted that student–faculty interaction has received nearly universal support as a means of enhancing the undergraduate experience. However, students often still operate with the expectation that the instructor will be the sage on the stage and the student role is simply to rather passively attempt to absorb as much of the knowledge being shared as possible through note-taking followed by rote memorization for an exam. Clouder and Deepwell (2004) concluded that instructors need to convince students that they can construct knowledge that is of value. Students' willingness to actively engage in this process is tied to their perceptions of the instructor and the classroom environment (Myers and Claus 2012), that is, to their definition of the situation. As we discussed in Chapter 2, it is on the first day of class that instructors have the best opportunity to influence students' perceptions and convince them that they are co-creators of learning in the classroom.

By engaging students in a discussion about discussion, being explicit about expectations for student participation and your motives for that expectation, you help students to construct a new definition of the classroom. You might ask students, "What do you think is my motivation for required participation in discussion?" Explain, as we noted in Chapter 1, that the research suggests students will learn more and will develop critical thinking skills more effectively if they are actively engaged in the classroom. You, as a result of your education, training, and experience have an advantage in some ways. But students can help each other learn and help you understand how best to assist them in the learning process. As one who has spent a lot of time and energy studying your subject matter, you have become an expert. An expert has such a high degree of facility with the subject that many aspects of the analysis of performance are second nature and taken for granted. Thus it is difficult for an expert to remember what it's like to be a novice learner. Your students can help you see where you are skipping over taken-for-granted steps in logic or in a problem-solving process. They can show one another how to make connections that you as the instructor may inadvertently take for granted because of your familiarity with the material.

One variation on this discussion about discussion is to ask students to share their best and worst experiences with classroom discussions. Without using names of instructors or courses, ask students to describe bad and good discussion experiences. What did the instructor do and what did the students do in each scenario? Which approaches made for good-versus-bad discussion experiences? How did instructors facilitate effective discussions and how did they sometimes inadvertently undermine the effectiveness of discussion? By keeping track of the classroom characteristics students describe, you can rather quickly develop a template that can be used to build effective approaches for discussion in your course.

Your goal is always to help students learn and develop thinking skills. You are not introducing discussion as a learning strategy to make things easier for yourself. In fact, the opposite is likely true. It's much easier for you to maintain control through constant lecture than it is for you to release control and trust that students will be prepared and willing to effectively engage in the learning process. You are taking a risk as well. But participation in discussion also requires some risk on the part of students. You can assure them that you will do everything within your power to make the classroom environment safe for participation and to affirm students who take the risk of doing so. Learning often involves identifying and challenging taken-for-granted assumptions. This can be an uncomfortable process. It takes work to identify those assumptions and courage to question their accuracy.

Explain that students can help each other learn by being supportive and encouraging of each other as they all begin to recognize that often there is no single correct answer and that they can learn from others with whom they may disagree. By viewing a topic from multiple perspectives, each with some insight to contribute, they can develop a fuller understanding. Students need to recognize that in the college classroom they do not have a "right not to be challenged" (Trosset 1998). They have a right not to be personally attacked and a right to be treated with respect and fairness by their instructor and their classmates. But they should expect that beliefs and positions taken must be defended with logic and evidence.

Another point for a discussion about discussion is after the first discussion, hopefully during the first or second class meeting of a course. Ask students to stop and reflect on the collective learning that has just occurred. Perhaps a Think-Pair-Share is appropriate as you ask students, What did you find useful in the exchange we just had? If an absent classmate asked you to summarize what went on in class and what you learned, how would you respond? What could we, as a class, do during future meetings to make discussions more productive and fruitful? If you had to grade today's discussion, what grade would you assign and why? Asking students to reflect upon their learning and the process of learning immediately following the first discussion in a course both helps students redefine their understanding of their role in the class and causes them to begin to assess their own learning and how to increase it. You are also humanizing yourself by making clear that even though you are the expert in the classroom, you can benefit from students' input to facilitate learning.

By being explicit with students about your expectations for interaction and how they should treat one another during inter-actions along with an explanation of the associated learning goals, instructors can help students redefine the college classroom. We can help move students from holding a definition wherein they expect the instructor to be the sage on the stage to one wherein they are responsible, at least in part, for their own and their class-mates' learning. In addition to having a discussion about discussion, it's important to consider what your syllabus communicates to students about your expectation for their engagement.

Using the Syllabus to Redefine the Classroom

How does your syllabus lead to a particular definition of your course? Perhaps the best way to approach this is to consider how you balance the dominant *syllabus as a contract* between instructor and students approach with a view of the *syllabus as an invitation* to an exciting adventure together. I am quite sympathetic to the need to ensure one's syllabus includes all of the appropriate university policies. (For a listing of key elements, see Greenwood and Howard 2011, 85). As a dean who sometimes has to deal with student claims of unfair treatment by faculty members, I know how important it is for faculty to clearly spell out expectations for student work and behavior and the penalties associated with missed, incomplete, or late work, for example. These are necessary to ensure the fair treatment of both students and faculty members. However, an ideal syllabus is more than a contract.

A syllabus should also be an invitation that motivates and encourages students to participate in an exciting, collective process of learning material and developing skills. Certainly, one way to do this is through the course description. Perhaps you are required by departmental or university policy to use the standard and (often) stiff, formal language of an officially approved course description. But you are not necessarily required to limit yourself to that language. You can follow the official course description with your interpretation of that language explaining why the content is important and how you will go about approaching it in order to facilitate student achievement of learning objectives.

For example, the description for the introductory course in sociology at my institution reads rather formally:

> **Understanding Society:** An exploration of key concepts, research methods and theoretical perspectives in sociology applied to a specific topic, theme or set of topics. Concepts covered include: culture, socialization, deviance, social structure, social stratification and inequality (including class, race and gender), and social institutions.

Admittedly, that sounds like contractual language about the topics to be covered in a course. Therefore on my syllabus I add my own description of the course using language that I hope sounds much like an invitation to an adventure of discovery:

> We eventually learn, despite what we may have been taught to expect as we grew up, that in many ways life is not fair. Some people are born into positions of advantage and others are born into lives where the deck is stacked against them. This doesn't mean that one's fate is predetermined, but success in life comes much more easily for some than it does for others who have

more obstacles to overcome in order to achieve at the same level. *Understanding Society* is a course that will allow you to investigate the many and surprising ways we are influenced by the groups to which we belong, and the interaction that takes place in those groups. We will do so through an exploration of key concepts, research methods, and theoretical perspectives of sociology and apply them to the topic of inequalities in society. Often inequalities exist along racial, gender, and social class lines. But inequalities also show up in ways we don't normally think about, such as with regard to one's level of attractiveness.

Another means of making the syllabus more like an invitation to something exciting and worthwhile is to organize the schedule not by topics using disciplinary jargon that students may not understand, but rather with the big questions: Why are you covering a given topic? What importance does it have for the field and for the student? What question are you attempting to answer with your exploration of a given day's topic? In my own experience teaching sociology, instead of using a heading like "Culture," I use the question, "How Did Humans Become the Dominant Species on the Planet?" Then, on the day(s) we cover the topic, I make the argument that the answer is through the development of culture. Instead of calling the day's topic "Social Structure," I ask the question, "How Is Society Possible?" The question, "Is Life Fair?" is a much more engaging invitation than using the heading "Social Stratification"—terminology most introductory students will not understand. Each of these questions suggests that together we will be engaged in a process of answering important and interesting questions that matter to students, rather than merely learning the jargon of the discipline. It feels much more like an invitation to a conversation and signals to students' that their participation will be required to answer these questions.

A third way the syllabus communicates expectations for student engagement is through the structuring of activities. Fassinger (1996) stresses the importance of designing a course structure that will allow students to interact with each other, bolster their confidence, and set a pattern of engagement throughout the semester. If the structure described in the syllabus suggests that the course consists entirely of instructor-focused lectures followed by objective examinations, a message regarding student passivity is being sent. Alternatively, the course structure could include group work in class or outside of class, which sends a message of engagement. Will all forms of assessment of student learning be individual assessments or will the course include assessments of group work? Will the instructor make participation a component of the final course grade? Or will it be used to determine a student's grade when otherwise it falls on the bubble between grade levels? We address the pros and cons of grading student participation in discussion in Chapter 6. But for now, it is sufficient to say that how you structure your course and how you describe that structure in the syllabus communicates a message to students regarding your expectations for participation. Be certain that you are communicating a message you want students to hear.

Impact of the Physical Environment on Definitions of the Classroom

The physical context for a course also contributes to a particular definition of the situation. Students have familiarity with a range of classroom environments. For example, they have likely been in auditorium-like classrooms with fixed rows of seats facing a stage at the front where the faculty member stands behind a podium. The physical facilities in this case certainly encourage students to think of the classroom as one that will feature a sage on the stage and require very little of them in terms of participation. This may be the case even when furniture is movable, say tablet-arm chairs, but still arranged in rows facing the front of the room. In circumstances such as this, instructors need to recognize that the classroom environment contributes to students' initial definitions of the situation. The room itself may be telling students that the focus is on the instructor; the student's job is to passively observe and take notes.

Consider how a laboratory classroom communicates something quite different to students. If students are arranged around lab benches with sinks and gas lines or around workspaces beneath fume hoods, it tells students that they are going to be required to actively do something. This is not a class where students will passively focus on the sage on the stage at the front of the room. They are expected to be active participants.

Therefore, whenever possible, it's a good idea for an instructor to arrange classroom furniture as one way of communicating a particular definition of the situation in the classroom to students. On the first day of class, if the faculty member has arrived early and rearranged the furniture into a circle or a horseshoe, it signals that in this course students will be expected to interact with each other as well as interact with the faculty member. As noted previously, a seating arrangement that allows students to see one another's faces increases students' confidence to request clarification because they can see peers' body language and expressions that assure them that they are not the only ones needing clarification. If the physical environment of your classroom is not flexible, as noted in the previous chapter, an instructor can still put students seated near each other into pairs or small groups to attempt to counter the message given by the classroom layout. If you are in a large classroom where it is simply not possible to rearrange furniture, you can change where you stand in the classroom. Move from side to side if you are trapped in the front by the furniture. Even better, move up and down rows or aisles in the classroom to reduce the distance between instructor and students. You can also arrive early to class and welcome students with a friendly greeting. This can change the tenor of the class and help you overcome the limitations of the classroom arrangement. Changing what you do in the classroom, can communicate a different message even if you cannot change the layout of the classroom.

Structuring the Course to Redefine the Classroom

There are a wide variety of pedagogical strategies faculty members can use to help shape the definition of the classroom and students' roles within it. If our objective is to develop the type of critical thinking, deep structure learning that Roberts (2002) suggests, then a shift from lecture to engagement through discussion makes sense. Discussion is one of the most commonly used pedagogical strategies to promote student engagement that can lead to greater long-term retention, motivation to learn, application of knowledge, and development of thinking skills (see Bonwell and Eison 1991 for a summary). But these benefits are not gained automatically or easily. Students' perceptions of their peers matter as much or more than their perceptions of their instructor (Hirschy and Wilson 2002) in their willingness to participate in active learning. A sense of connection to classroom peers can increase students' willingness to be engaged (Sidelinger and Booth-Butterfield 2010).

Students are more engaged in courses where the instructor both signals openness to student participation as well as signals that he or she views the faculty role to be helping students to succeed (Gasiewski et al. 2012). If we can convince students we are on their side, seeking their success while simultaneously upholding an appropriate standard for learning, we can help them redefine the classroom as a situation that requires their active participation. When students adopt a sense of ownership for their own learning and perceive their classmates are affirming of them, they are more willing to be actively engaged (Sidelinger 2010). Therefore, as previously noted, it's important to structure a course in a way that helps students develop positive connections early in the semester.

Another instructor strategy is to simply know one's students (see Greenwood and Howard 2011). Understanding whether your students work in addition to attending college, whether they have children, if they are first-generation college students, what their interests are, and so forth can help an instructor know how best to engage them. When you take the time to learn about your students, you have the opportunity to adapt your course to better meet their needs. Braxton, Eimers, and Bayer (1996) suggest using examples in class and giving assignments that are based on students' interests and characteristics. For example, if you find that your introductory statistics course is largely populated by pharmacy majors, then using examples relevant to the experiences of future pharmacists is a means of making statistics more engaging to them.

Among the other ways to structure a course to ensure a definition of the classroom that includes students' active engagement is to tie reading assignments to discussion. Lewis and Hanc (2012) found that connecting readings to discussion increased the likelihood of students' reading the assignment and, therefore, being better prepared to contribute to their own and their classmates' learning. In a nine-semester study of my introductory sociology students, I (Howard 2005) also found that tying readings to in-class small-group discussions and just-in-time quizzes increased students' reading of the assignments.

In a study assessing the use of student response systems, or clickers, in the classroom, Smith et al. (2009) found that structuring the course in a way that utilized peer discussion could lead to improved understanding even when none of the students in a group originally knew the correct answer. Smith et al.'s (2009) approach communicates to students a definition of the classroom that suggests students need to take responsibility for being co-creators of their own and their classmates' understanding. Similarly, in a study that compared a course design focused on small-group activities and inquiry labs, Gill (2011) found that students were more engaged than their peers in comparison groups with more traditional lecture-based approaches. However, when asked to report which activities were most important for their learning, the students cited not the small-group activities or inquiry labs, but rather the lecture and video presentations.

Gill's (2011) finding reinforces the importance of having a discussion about discussion. Students who have been trained to perceive lecture as the primary or most important means of transmitting knowledge may not recognize the value of more interactive pedagogical strategies. It is important, therefore, to explain the rationale for the pedagogical strategies adopted by an instructor in order to help students begin to understand the benefits of engagement activities. It is also important to end discussions with a summary of learning. The instructor can simply ask the class, "What did we learn through the discussion today?" And then write key points on the board as they are raised by students, which will facilitate student note-taking and reflection upon the learning that has just occurred.

Institutional Support: An Aside

Clearly some of these challenges are more effectively addressed at an institutional rather than an individual level. If the climate of the campus is one wherein teaching and learning are taken seriously and faculty are rewarded and recognized for valuing teaching and learning, it is more likely that the definition of the classroom you are attempting to communicate to students will be reinforced frequently by other faculty members in their classrooms (Braxton, Eimers, and Bayer 1996). Reason, Terenzini, and Domingo (2006) have made a compelling argument for the importance of the institution's academic culture in supporting intellectual rigor and the expectation for high levels of student effort and commitment to academic work.

Umbach and Wawrzynski (2005), using two national data sets, concluded that students report greater engagement and learning at institutions where faculty members more frequently utilize active and collaborative learning techniques. But widespread faculty adoption of such approaches is not likely to happen without institutional support. Weaver and Qi (2005) suggest that while teaching and learning may still be prioritized at the typical liberal arts college, this is not always the case at larger, public institutions with a corresponding research mission. They maintain that only by developing and sustaining an organizational structure that recognizes and rewards a commitment to teaching and learning can an institution hope to inspire faculty to prioritize student learning. Likewise, if the institutional decision makers are committed to creating classrooms wherein the physical environment communicates an expectation for active learning, it is much easier for faculty members to influence students' definitions of the situation. So while this is an aside from direct discussion of classroom practice, it is a good idea for faculty members who value teaching and learning to seek to participate in governance structures where decisions are made that influence how classrooms are designed and furnished as well as defining how faculty activities are rewarded and valued. This may mean that you choose to involve yourself in service activities that are directly related to the teaching mission of your institution. It may mean that you actively support others who share these values or serve as a department chair or a faculty senator, for example, in order to advocate for these priorities. In some cases it may mean that a faculty member who values teaching and learning may have to find a position at an institution where one's personal commitment and values are best aligned with that of the institution.

Conclusion

While students may enter our classrooms with a definition of the situation that is less than ideal, the story does not have to end there. Savvy faculty members can take intentional steps to enter into a negotiated redefinition of the classroom. We can do this through a discussion about discussion, the contents of our syllabi, the physical environment of the classroom, and the way we structure our courses. While individual faculty members can help redefine the classroom in their own courses, it is a job made much easier, more effectively widespread, and more profitable in the long term when there is strong support from the institutional structure as well.

When students' definitions of the classroom are aligned with those of the instructor, you are much less likely to develop sweaty palms worrying about contradictory comments on the course evaluation form. Such contradictory comments are quite common. You are not alone. Hopefully this chapter has equipped you with an understanding and pedagogical strategies that will align students' expectations with your own and lead to fewer contradictory comments related to participation and discussion. In Chapter 5 we turn to another approach that benefits greatly from institutional support: utilizing online environments for student engagement.

5

Making Online Discussion Work

You did it. A few semesters ago, you took the plunge, moved outside of your comfort zone, and added an online discussion forum to your class. You heard about how the online forums encourage those quiet and shy students who rarely, if ever, speak up in your class to contribute to discussions and how the quality of the discussions is supposed to improve because students have time to reflect, and perhaps even look things up, before contributing to the dialogue. You smartly linked the discussion forums to the reading assignments. Things went slowly at first as students seemed reluctant to initiate discussions and to respond to each other's posts. So the next semester you added "discussion starter" questions to help students with their reflections on the readings. You also made participation in the forums a course requirement. But too frequently a majority of the students waited until shortly before the deadline to post their comments, undermining any opportunity for student-to-student exchange. So you revised things once again by creating two deadlines. The first required students to post a comment by Thursday and the second required a response to a classmate's post by the forum's close on Sunday.

This iterative process has helped. Now the vast majority of students are posting and responding to classmates in the online forums as you have mandated. But that seems to be about all they are doing—meeting the minimum requirements. Aren't these students supposed to be the "eGeneration," familiar with and comfortable interacting in an online environment, and perhaps even preferring online to face-to-face interactions? Frankly, while things are not terrible, you expected more from them.

And then there's the issue of the benefit of the online discussion forums versus the cost to you as instructor. Sometimes there are hundreds of posts to skim through and grade. Shouldn't you read each post, if for no other reason than to ensure students are following proper netiquette and treating each other respectfully? But how do you move students away from the superficial "I agree with what she said" type of responses into something more substantive without taking over the forums yourself? Reading all those posts is not only a headache for you, some students seem quite resentful that they are required to read them, too. And you're getting those same mixed reviews on your course evaluations. Some students praise the forums as beneficial for their learning and others complain they are a waste of time. You wonder, is online discussion all it's cracked up to be?

How Many Students Participate in Online Learning?

Online discussion can be a component of a traditional face-to-face college course or a course that is taught entirely online. In either case, we need to be aware of effective pedagogical practice for facilitating learning through discussion that occurs online. Online courses are increasingly available to students, and students at many types of institutions, from community colleges to small liberal arts colleges to large public universities, are often choosing to enroll in online courses. According to the Survey of Online Learning, in 2011 there were over 6.7 million students taking at least one online course, which equates to 32 percent of all higher education students (Allan and Seaman 2013). The growth rate for students taking online courses continues to far outpace the overall growth rate in higher education. Without a doubt, online education is here to stay and likely to become ever more prevalent at colleges and universities around the country and around the world.

While we often think there is a simple dichotomy between online and face-to-face courses, it is more accurate to think of a continuum in course delivery options. In the Survey of Online Learning (Allan and Seaman 2013), there are four types of courses defined by the percentage of content that is delivered online. *Traditional* courses are defined as those using no online technology; all content is delivered in writing or orally. *Web-facilitated* courses deliver up to 29 percent of the content online, typically using a *course management system* (CMS) to enhance what is essentially a traditional face-to-face course. Instructors may post syllabi and assignments or utilize an online discussion forum in the CMS. *Blended/hybrid* courses deliver 30 to 79 percent of the content online. In a blended/hybrid course substantial content is delivered both face-to-face and online, often with a reduced number of face-to-face class meetings. Finally, an *online* course is defined as one where most or all of the content is delivered online and typically there are no face-to-face meetings. Increasingly institutions are not only offering courses online, but entire degree programs online (Allan and Seaman 2013). Also there is the issue of the *massive open online courses* (MOOCs), one type of online course. Some fear that MOOCs offered by highly prestigious research institutions will put many small colleges out of business in the coming decades if someone comes up with a way to generate significant revenue through MOOCs. Others see MOOCs as a fad that is getting more attention than deserved. But regardless of the impact of MOOCs, there is no doubt that online learning is and will continue to be an increasingly popular option.

This tremendous growth in online learning suggests that we need to pay careful attention to pedagogical issues related to online delivery. Online discussion can happen in a web-facilitated course, a blended/hybrid course, or an online course. While I have not been able to find research that identifies the number or percentage of higher education students taking courses that require participation in online discussion as a part of a face-to-face course, by definition, it is likely much higher than the 32 percent of all higher education students who take at least one online course. How can instructors utilize discussions to promote effective learning for these students in the online environment?

The Flipped Classroom: What Does Good Online Pedagogy Look Like?

Online courses and online course components need to be interactive and engaging in order to best facilitate learning. As Stewart, Bachman, and Babb (2009) concluded, "If courses are nothing more than content, then all students would need is their textbook" (p. 511). As faculty we need to be adding value to the classroom that goes beyond merely presenting content. The old assumption that if a faculty member is a content expert, then he or she is prepared to teach that content is no longer adequate. Faculty need to give careful thought to their pedagogical choices in order to facilitate students' learning. Well-informed faculty members know that learning is an active process that is enhanced through collaboration with others, including the faculty member as well as peers.

In some ways this runs counter to the *flipped classroom* model, where content is placed online in the form of readings and/or videos of lectures and face-to-face time is spent in interactive activities with the instructor and classmates. Svinicki (2013) argues that flipped classrooms are not as easy as they might appear. Rather than an instructor spending time providing new information during class time, a flipped classroom requires that students spend time outside of class preparing for in-class activities. This could simply be a matter of students completing reading assignments ahead of time or perhaps watching a video of a lecture. The challenge, of course, is ensuring that students are preparing by completing the out-of-class assignments. Svinicki (2013) even suggests that rather than an in-class lecture, a video, or a self-study computer lesson would probably be a more effective learning experience (p. 12).

While I absolutely agree that the engagement of students during face-to-face sessions is a good strategy for promoting learning, the rather passive form in which content is likely to be delivered online (e.g., a video of a lecture) is not an ideal approach to promoting learning. There is something to be said for an interactive lecture that engages students as new content is being introduced as compared to students attempting to absorb new content on their own through technology without the active guidance of a faculty member. In his reflections on experimenting with a flipped classroom, Talbert (2014b) laments that students in a flipped classroom may rebel because they prefer lecture as it better enables them to understand how to earn an A in the course. He notes that in a flipped classroom there is likely plenty of lecturing going on—it's just been moved online in a video-based format. While Talbert (2014b) at least implies that students are merely pursuing grades ("Tell me what I need to memorize for the exam and I will do so") rather than learning, I would like to offer a different interpretation of students' preference for lecture in a face-to-face classroom as opposed to lecture via an online video.

In another in his series of insightful columns reflecting on experiences with a flipped classroom, Talbert (2014a) rejects a comment on his blog that claimed students are unable to learn the content on their own. He argues that the most important things we learn in life (e.g., speaking and reading; potty training; feeding oneself; walking; listening to and interpreting others' statements) are things we learn on our own through a trial-and-error process. At the risk of reducing Talbert's thoughtful attempts to struggle with developing effective approaches to the flipped classroom to a straw-man argument, the sociologist in me strongly objects to his conclusion and suggests that the opposite is true.

While we have the inherited the potential to learn to speak, to walk, or to go to the bathroom unassisted, whether or not that potential is realized is heavily dependent upon socialization—our interactions with others. We obviously cannot learn to speak a language without the benefit of interacting with others in that trial-and-error process. We achieve our potential to walk because someone is both modeling walking for us and holding our hand as we attempt to take those first steps. Might we learn to walk without the help of others? Perhaps we could, but it is neither likely nor certain that we would. Learning to walk without the help of others would be immensely more difficult. So I think Talbert (2014a) is drawing the wrong conclusion. The most important learning and the most effective learning happens through a social process. And learning through lecture is also a social experience. It might be learning in a comparatively passive manner but it is still social—someone has to be assisting us by delivering the lecture (even if it is mediated by technology). So when students complain that they prefer face-to-face lecture instead of online lectures in a flipped classroom, they are not indicating a preference for passive learning. Rather they are indicating a preference for the opportunity to engage in interactive learning. So implying that students' preference for face-to-face lecture over an online recording of a lecture is about pursuing grades is misleading. Students recognize they learn content more effectively and more quickly when they have the opportunity to interact with the faculty member.

In a flipped classroom with a digital recording of a lecture, there is no opportunity to ask questions. There is unlikely to be a pause where the instructor asks students to apply content just explained to their own experiences. Students cannot interrupt and say, "I'm confused. Can you explain that again?" Presenting content in an interactive lecture in a face-to-face setting is, in my view, significantly better than an online presentation of content through a digitized lecture that encourages students to be passive recipients of knowledge.

In an online video lecture, one runs the risk of inadvertently encouraging students to adopt the "banking model of education" wherein the instructor is the bank of knowledge and students make withdrawals by taking notes as the instructor speaks (Freire 2006).

On the positive side, the rather passive forms of online delivery of content can be utilized as a preparation, however imperfect, for the in-class interaction that develops a fuller understanding of the content. But as instructors we should always be asking ourselves, what is the added value that I bring to the classroom and how can I use student engagement strategies to help students maximize the benefit of what I bring to the course? I can read students' body language and sense when they are failing to grasp what I just presented. I can shift my approach on the spot and offer a different example in hopes of clarifying. I can repeat myself, emphasizing an important point that I or my students may have glossed over too quickly. The social nature of the face-to-face classroom makes these adaptations more readily possible.

Svinicki (2013) astutely recognizes that one reason students may not read material prior to class is that they utilize the in-class presentation as an "advance organizer" that better helps them learn from the readings that are completed later. While I am advocating throughout this book for an interactive, discussion-focused classroom, I also think that lecture as a pedagogical strategy often gets less than it is due. I recognize that not all lectures are the same. Sometimes a lecture amounts to the instructor being a walking, talking human highlighter that merely signals for students what content found in the textbook will be most likely to show up on the exam. However, a lecture can be much more than that. An interactive presentation of material through lecture, ripe with helpful illustrations and opportunities for students to ask questions and apply what they are learning, can be an effective learning experience. Of course, figuring out how to effectively present an interactive online lecture is challenging.

In an interesting attempt to adapt lessons from Ken Bain's (2004) influential *What the Best College Teachers Do* to the online learning environment, Brinthaupt et al. (2011) note that the best college teachers foster student engagement with their peers, their instructor, and the content while seeing the potential for learning in every student and striving to foster students' intrinsic motivation. Bain (2004, 99–103) concludes that in this approach faculty create a natural learning environment for students that includes five critical elements: (1) a provocative question or problem; (2) guiding students to appreciate the significance of the question; (3) encouraging critical thinking; (4) creating an environment that supports the students in attempts to address the question; and (5) leaving the students with additional questions and a desire to know more. Brinthaupt et al. (2011) rightly argue that none of these five critical elements are contingent upon delivery method. Instructors can utilize any of a number of tools to create a natural online learning environment, and discussion forums are one of those important tools.

Synchronous versus Asynchronous Online Discussion

Online discussion forums occur in two formats: synchronous or asynchronous. In synchronous discussions, all learners are online simultaneously engaging in real-time conversation that often takes place in a chat room within a course management system (CMS). While synchronous discussions have the advantage of getting immediate feedback to one's posts, simply finding a time when all learners can be online simultaneously can be quite a challenge. Technological difficulties can also haunt synchronous online discussions. If the discussion is scheduled for a one-hour period at a specified time and date, but multiple students have difficulty accessing the chat room because of technological issues, either with the CMS or with the student's Internet access or computer, the benefits of real-time interaction are lost for those students. It can also be challenging to follow a synchronous online discussion because multiple students are attempting to join in the conversation simultaneously; it's difficult to type one's input while also keeping track of others' input as it pops up on the screen.

Synchronous discussions can also head down multiple tracks simultaneously, leading to confusion as students are attempting to participate in a conversation that has splintered into two or more directions. These challenges make synchronous online discussions less straightforward than one might think.

One of the key benefits of online learning is flexibility. Many students choose online learning options because of the scheduling flexibility. Students may have job-related responsibilities or child-care responsibilities that make their availability for class at a set time quite challenging. Requiring synchronous discussions, by definition, takes away this benefit for students. Therefore, if one is going to require synchronous discussions as part of an online class or as an online component of a traditional face-to-face course, at the very least the instructor should clearly indicate on the syllabus, and prior to the start of the course, exactly when participation in synchronous discussions will be required and what the penalties are for failure to participate. This courtesy allows students the option of withdrawing from the course if they are unavailable to participate in the synchronous discussion. Given these challenges, asynchronous discussions are more typically utilized in online formats.

Asynchronous online discussions do not require that all learners be online simultaneously interacting in real time. By allowing students to post in a discussion forum at their convenience, students are given greater opportunity to consider a topic and perhaps even conduct their own research prior to posting. Du, Durrington, and Matthews (2007) found that students preferred to have time to reflect prior to posting in online discussions. Some have concluded that asynchronous discussions provide students more information and lead to more meaningful analyses than discussion in the traditional classroom (see, for example, Al-Shalchi 2009). While online asynchronous discussions allow for the possibility that students will prepare more thoughtful comments and could do research in advance of posting, this should not be taken as a given. To date, there is no systematic research that attempts to carefully assess the quality and depth of student comments in online versus face-to-face discussions.

Student Learning in Online versus Face-to-Face Courses

Before we can analyze the effectiveness of online discussion forums for facilitating student learning, it is helpful to first consider the research evidence related to online learning more generally. Are online courses as effective in promoting student learning as approaches typically found in the face-to-face classroom? Most studies comparing student learning outcomes in traditional and online courses have found very little in the way of difference. For example, Ary and Brune (2011) found no significant difference in student performance in traditional and online Personal Finance courses. In an intriguing longitudinal study of 30 sections of the same course taught both online and face-to-face from 2001 to 2010, Wagner, Garippo, and Lovaas (2011) found no significant difference in student learning between the two modes of delivery. While these are examples of the most common research strategy, comparing online and face-to-face sections of the same course taught by the same instructor, there have also been multiple attempts to review the hundreds of studies concerning learning in online versus face-to-face courses and draw conclusions.

In a meta-analysis of 232 comparative studies published from 1985–2002, Bernard et al. (2004) also found very little in the way of statistically significant differences between online and traditional courses. When it comes to facilitating student learning, in some cases online courses outperformed the face-to-face courses; in just as many cases the opposite was true. However, when examining synchronous (such as two groups of students in different locations being connected by some form of technology, e.g., a video link, and taught simultaneously) and asynchronous (wherein students in remote locations work independently or in asynchronous groups) strategies, Bernard et al. (2004) found that synchronous applications favored traditional classroom instruction while asynchronous applications favored distance education, but noted there was still wide variability.

Shachar and Neumann (2010) also conducted a meta-analysis of research that estimated and compared differences in academic performance of students enrolled in distance education courses with those in traditional courses. They examined the results of 129 studies conducted from 1990 to 2009. Shachar and Neumann (2010) found that in 70 percent of the studies, students taking distance education courses outperformed their peers in traditional courses. There was an upward trend in overall advantage for online courses in the period 2000–2009, suggesting that perhaps instructors are learning to be more effective in their online teaching and that students are becoming more comfortable with online learning over time. One caution to keep in mind here is that in virtually all of the studies there is no random assignment of students to either online or face-to-face courses. Students typically self-select the course in which they enroll. So it is possible that more motivated or higher-achieving students chose to enroll in one type of course or the other. Few studies attempt to control for the level of students' preparation or motivation for a given course.

But our concern is not so much with learning in online courses in general as with the discussion that occurs in an online con-text. The research suggests that online instruction is at least as effective as face-to-face instruction in terms of student learning outcomes. But our question is more specific. What about online discussion? Can we reasonably conclude, as with online courses in general, online discussion leads to similar outcomes as discussion in face-to-face settings? Do the same norms that guide student behav-ior in the classroom setting impact discussions when they take place online? If we want to engage students in interactions with each other, their instructor, and the material in an online format, what steps can we take to maximize the learning outcomes? What does the research tell us that can inform our efforts to facilitate learning in an online setting? While there is much less research examining learning in online discussion forums specifically, we can still draw some at least tentative answers to these questions and identify some best practices for discussion forums in an online format.

Online Discussion Norms

While the norms that guide participation in online discussions are not well researched and documented, it appears that the norms of civil attention and consolidation of responsibility do not operate in the same way or to the same extent in online discussion forums as compared to face-to-face classrooms. This is largely due to the fact that, frequently, participation in online discussion forums is a course requirement. Requiring participation of all students removes the possibility of students merely paying civil attention. Instead students must actually pay attention and engage in the discussion forums. Required participation likewise greatly reduces the chances that a few students will accept responsibility for participation in online discussion while others become free-riders. Nonetheless, norms in online courses, just like those in face-to-face courses, are always in an ongoing process of negotiation between the instructor and students (Hewling 2005).

In a study of 127 students in an online course on physiotherapy, Clouder and Deepwell (2004) divided students into six groups for discussion in online forums. They found that the majority of students were not motivated to contribute to discussion forums and were reluctant to initiate discussions. When students did post, their comments were not particularly worthwhile. Clouder and Deepwell (2004) concluded that students in online courses, just like those in face-to-face courses, need to be persuaded that they can be active participants in the construction of knowledge and understanding in a manner that is valuable to all course participants, including themselves. Their study suggests that apart from requiring participation in online discussion forums, instructors may encounter the problems of civil attention and the consolidation of responsibility with the majority leaving participation in the discussion forums in the hands of a few students. However, it appears that many, if not most, online instructors have chosen to make participation in online forums a course requirement that is a part of one's grade as opposed to an optional activity. Grading participation in an online forum therefore reduces the chances that most students will be silent and allow a few dominant talkers (or posters) to account for the vast majority of student input. Given this structure, can an instructor assume that all students are likely to participate at a roughly equal rate?

Student Demographics and Online Participation

There is some very limited and tentative evidence of demographic variation in students' perceptions of and participation in online discussion forums. However, any conclusions must be viewed with caution as much of the research is based on very small samples of students, often at the graduate level, which may or may not represent the typical undergraduate experience in online discussion.

Ashong and Commander (2012) in a study of 120 graduate and undergraduate students enrolled in online courses at a large research university found that while students generally have positive perceptions of online learning, female students held more positive views compared to male students. They also found that white students had more positive views of asynchronous discussion than did African Americans. A few studies have suggested that female students may participate more frequently and have more positive views of and/or greater motivation with regard to online discussions (Abbad and Albarghouthi 2011; Anderson and Simpson 2004; Jahng, Nielsen, and Chan 2010). In one study, Shackelford and Maxwell (2012) found that age and gender differences did not affect the sense of community online.

In terms of learning outcomes in online courses, Ryabov (2012) found some evidence that female students outperformed male students in online sociology courses. Sher (2008) examined student learning in a variety of online courses and found no significant differences by academic area. In a study of the impact of professional experience on participation in asynchronous online discussion forums, Cornacchione et al. (2012) found no significant difference in the number of posts by novice and expert students. But all in all, such studies are few and typically utilize a small sample of courses and/or students taught by only one or a few instructors. Therefore, it is very difficult to draw any conclusions about the impact of demographic variables on participation in online discussion forums.

Online Discussion and Student Learning

Judging by the number of articles published offering advice for best practices, online discussion forums are a very commonly utilized pedagogical strategy. In a yearlong study of use of a course management system at Brigham Young University, discussion boards were in the top three pedagogical features utilized by instructors and students (Griffiths and Graham 2009). Kearns (2012), in a study of 24 online courses, found that online discussion was the second most frequently utilized assessment strategy after written assignments. Kearns (2012) also found that the average weight assigned to participation in online discussion was 32 percent of the total course grade, although the range was wide (4–80%). As noted earlier, making participation in online discussion a part of the course grade certainly has the potential to increase participation. Al-Shalchi (2009) argued that at times it is possible to get greater participation in online discussion forums than in face-to-face classrooms. The level of participation, of course, will be greatly influenced by the instructor's choice of pedagogical strategies regardless of the course delivery system—online or face-to-face.

So while we can safely conclude that online discussion forums, at least when they are a component of the course grade, get students participating, what is the quality of their discussion? O'Neal (2009) found that the quality of discussion in online and face-to-face courses is similar when content-related questions are used to structure discussions. In a study of an online graduate course, Ruan and Griffith (2011) found that online discussion strengthens the sense of learning community, facilitates sharing of professional experience, and enhances teacher reflection. This suggests that in professional programs where students are already likely to be employed in their field, online discussion forums can have particular benefits for such students.

Students perceive they are achieving at higher levels when online interactions are an important component of a course (Jiang 1998). In a study of freshmen composition students, discussion boards were helpful when it came to basic skills such as clarifying topic, purpose, and thesis statements, but less helpful in higher-order thinking challenges such as developing counterarguments (Bacabac 2010). Despite this finding, we need to be careful not to assume that online discussions are always less effective at promoting those higher-order thinking skills. As we know, face-to-face discussions don't automatically result in higher-order thinking, either. Much depends on the use of effective pedagogical choices and strategies designed to both engage students and facilitate their higher-order thinking. In a comparison of discussion in online and face-to-face courses, Blanchette (2001) found that the online students used more rhetorical questions to persuade, think aloud, and challenge others as well as demonstrated higher levels of cognition overall than their face-to-face peers.

In a study of the online behaviors of 98 undergraduate students in an online business course, Hung and Zhang (2008) found numerous interesting patterns. Students accessed course material more often than they interacted with the instructor or peers online.

Not surprisingly, students read messages more frequently than post messages. Despite the heavy emphasis on peer collaboration in the course, the most common behaviors were relatively passive ones—accessing or reading course materials posted online. Hung and Zhang (2008) were able to correlate online behaviors with student performance and found that, indeed, both the frequency of accessing course materials and the number of messages in online forums read were important predictors of student performance. So despite being relatively passive actions compared to direct interaction with their peers, these students were engaging with the content by accessing course materials and reading peers' posts. In addition, more active-learner behaviors, including the number of messages posted by a student and the number of synchronous discussions in which they participated, also were positively correlated with performance in the course. Hung and Zhang (2008) concluded that their results clearly showed that active participation in the online discussions was more important in predicting student performance than simply reading learning materials.

In a study of online sociology courses, Ryabov (2012) found that time spent online and previous achievements were the two most important predictors of student performance. In this case, time spent online included time reading the assignments, as the only way students could access course readings was to read them online, an atypical approach. In fact, half of the time Ryabov's students were online was spent reading the assignments. Still Ryabov's finding is consistent with my own study (Howard 2005) of students in face-to-face sociology courses over nine semesters where the best predictors of performance were class attendance and reading of assignments.

In one of the few studies that directly examined the impact of participation in online discussion, Wolff and Dosdall (2010) found that such participation predicted both exam scores and course completion. Students who contributed little to discussion were 10 times more likely to not complete the course than their more-involved peers. This finding may seem obvious; if students are not completing one type of assignment in the course (posting in online forums), they are less likely to complete the course successfully. However, Wolff and Dosdall (2010) also found that among students who did complete the course, those who contributed little to online discussions scored lower on the final exam than their peers who were active participants in the forums. Of course, one could question the causal order of this finding. Is it the case that students learn more by participating in online forums or that better students are more likely to participate in online forums? Chances are that it is a case of both. Better students are more likely to participate in online forums and students who participate in those forums learn more than those who don't.

Given the research regarding face-to-face discussions that shows a few students will typically dominate the conversation, Wolff and Dosdall (2010) hypothesized that some students could become dominant talkers in online forums and through their over-participation thereby inhibit their own and their classmates' learning. However, their analysis did not find any point where the amount of participation in online discussion forums was so great that it had a negative impact on others' learning—thus they found no support for their hypothesis.

While the research clearly affirms that actively engaging students in online, collaborative discussion forums leads to improved performance, students do not necessarily or automatically embrace this pedagogical approach. Because of the ease and convenience, as well as their personal comfort level, students may prefer independent and passive modes of instruction in online courses (Cuthrell and Lyon 2007). Du, Durrington, and Matthews (2007) found that online students preferred to work alone on projects as opposed to working in groups. This was the case even though students recognized that their critical thinking skills were enhanced when they worked collaboratively. In their attempt to explain this seeming contradiction in their study, Du, Durrington, and Matthews (2007) discovered that students' preference for working alone was largely due to previous poor experiences collaborating with online peers. Those poor experiences may have been due to unmotivated peer collaborators or due to the difficulty in coordinating collaborative work in an online environment. The coordination challenges might result from issues with technology or simply from difficulties presented by the students' already crowded schedules. This finding points to the importance of instructors taking responsibility to structure online collaborative discussions in such a way as to maximize the potential for effectiveness and efficiency. So how do we structure online discussions to maximize learning?

Maximizing Effectiveness of Online Discussion

Online discussions tend to be threaded discussions wherein replies to an initial post are grouped together to allow for ease of reading and following a conversation on a particular topic. In an *online threaded discussion* instructor control needs to be balanced with learner control. Instructors should scaffold or structure the discussion forums in a way that will maximize participation and effectiveness without overwhelming students.

Group Size and Online Discussion

Peters (no date) suggests that no more than seven learners should be included in a group for an online discussion, allowing for all to participate and respond to each other's posts without creating an undue workload. She also argues that random assignment of students to groups is less effective than attempting to group students by major, interests, or other commonalities. A sense of social presence of both the instructor and students is important for creating a sense of community in online forums. One way to facilitate social presence is through the use of emoticons, something instructors can model for students in their posts (Peters no date). Tying online discussion forums to readings, class activities, and exams encourages students to read assignments and to view collaborative activities as learning experiences, and motivates learning. Peters (no date) advises requiring students post twice in each discussion forum with an earlier deadline for a comment and a later deadline for a reply to a classmate's post. When instructors take steps such as these, they are creating a structure, a scaffold that will encourage students to begin to learn from each other through their online interactions.

Increasing Quality of Forum Posts

One problem instructors may encounter in online discussion forums is also commonly found in face-to-face discussion groups. Students may be talking (or posting) a lot, but not saying much of value (Clouder and Deepwell 2004). Kearns (2012) found some instructors were frustrated with students' lack of deep engagement with the material and with other students in online forums. Rourke and Kanuka (2009), in a review of the literature, concluded that the vast majority of student posts in online forums represented only the lowest levels of cognition. Meyer (2004) and Schrire (2006) found somewhat greater evidence of higher-level cognition in online forums. Using Bloom's (1956) taxonomy as a means of assessing the extent to which students exhibit higher-order thinking skills, such as synthesis and evaluation, Ertmer, Sadaf, and Ertmer (2011) found that a mere 15 percent of student posts represented the highest levels of thinking. Other studies have found that the majority of student posts represent midlevel thinking, requiring analysis and application (Bradley et al. 2008; Christopher, Thomas, and Tallent-Runnels 2004). Again, a reminder is appropriate at this point. It is quite likely that the level of thinking demonstrated in online discussion forums is similar to that in face-to-face environments. It is likely that your personal experience affirms that face-to-face discussions often suffer from the same lower-order thinking. However, it is true that students participating in online discussion forums have the opportunity to think about and consider their posts, they have the opportunity to do some background research before participating, and they have the opportunity to write and revise before posting; therefore, superficial levels of thinking in online discussions are less excusable than in face-to-face settings where students must participate spontaneously. Yet, in both online and face-to-face discussions, the level of thinking students exhibit will have a lot to do with whether the instructor structures the discussion in a manner that facilitates higher-order thinking.

Another issue for instructors and students is that the threaded discussion that occurs in online forums often reads more like stream-of-consciousness writing or very rough first drafts, instead of carefully argued and polished essays (Greenlaw and DeLoach 2003). While students have the opportunity to research, write, and revise before posting, many will simply post spontaneous first drafts of their thinking. For example, in discussions, both face-to-face and online, students often jump to a conclusion without first building a case. So what can we do to ensure the highest possible quality of discussion in online formats?

Summarizing Online Discussions

One strategy is to require some type of post-discussion summary. Members of online discussion forum groups can be required to take turns writing a one-paragraph summary of conclusions based on the discussion in a forum. The instructor can then give a group grade based on the summary rather than attempting to grade each individual's contributions to a particular forum. These summaries, in addition to reducing the grading burden for the instructor, also provide a resource for students when preparing for exams or for use in writing assignments. Students can utilize the summary posts as a way of reviewing the material and the conclusions reached through online discussion.

Another strategy is for the instructor to model some nudging and direction through responses to students' posts. For example, an instructor might ask a group that is too quickly jumping to a conclusion without first building a case, "Upon what assumptions is your conclusion predicated? Are the assumptions reasonable or are they unfounded? If we make a different assumption, would you come to the same conclusion?" Similarly, the instructor can point out examples that run counter to the argument being made by students as a means of encouraging students to consider different perspectives. The goal in this situation is that students will learn to ask similar questions themselves as they begin to develop their own critical thinking skills.

However, in online discussion forums instructors must strive to remain the "guide on the side" rather than being the authority who intervenes to provide the "correct" answer. Chan, Hew, and Cheung (2009) found that when instructors resolve issues or summarize too quickly in online forums, the discussion can be prematurely cut off. Cooper (2009) found that in online discussion forums in math and science classes, there was tendency for discussion to abruptly cease once students perceived a correct solution had been posted. In these cases, it is important for instructors to provide probes that can help students, for example, understand the process of finding a solution. These studies also suggest that it should be a student member of the discussion forum group, not the professor, who does the summarizing of the discussion. A summary by the professor can be easily perceived as the definitive and final response to the question whereas students are likely to be more willing to offer additional comments and insights when another student posts the summary.

Building Online Community

While the quality of student posts in online forums can be disappointing to instructors, Hrastinski (2008) argues that even the "I agree with what she said" type of post has some value. Such comments help build social ties that are important for collaborative learning even if they contribute little to understanding the material immediately at hand. Of course, such affirming posts are more helpful early in the semester while a sense of community is being built as opposed to later in the semester after a sense of community has been established. By modeling the probing questions previously mentioned (What are your assumptions? Are those reasonable assumptions? What would you conclude if you made a different assumption? Can we cite evidence that runs counter to your conclusion?), instructors can encourage deeper levels of thinking in students' posts. Offering these questions in the syllabus as models for student replies to other students, encouraging the student replying to attempt to respond to these questions (as well as the original poster's comments), will lead to better quality online discussion.

Balancing the Workload in Online Discussion

Even when students are motivated and posting quality comments and questions in online discussion forums, there are still challenges that instructors must face. While mandatory participation can help avoid social loafing and the consolidation of responsibility for participation in discussion, the sheer number and length of posts can be problematic for both students and instructors (Baker 2011). If students become overwhelmed with the volume of posts they are expected to read, they may begin to merely skim through posts, read only until they find a post to which they can direct a simple reply, or stop reading them altogether. In Kearns's (2012) study of 24 online courses, students reported difficulties keeping up with reading their classmates' required posts in discussion forums. One simple way to address this issue for students is to follow Peters's (no date) advice and divide students into smaller groups, giving them fewer posts to read and to which they are expected to reply. However, this strategy doesn't solve the problem for the instructor, who may continue to feel compelled to monitor every post.

Several researchers (see, for example, Clarke 2011; Kearns 2012) have noted that not only can students feel overwhelmed as they attempt to keep up with posts in online discussions, so can instructors. Goldman (2012), in a study of instructors teaching online courses, found that more than 60 percent reported spending 7 to 12 hours per week reading and monitoring in discussion forums, averaging 10 hours per week on this task alone. While the vast majority of these instructors perceived the value of the online discussions to be "high" or "very high," reading and managing the forums constituted 65 percent of their total hours invested in the course. For students who also spent about 10 hours per week on the online forums, this constituted 55 percent of total student time spent on the course. However, students perceived the discussions to be less valuable than did their instructors with only 52 percent of learners ranking their value "high" or "very high" compared to 89 percent of instructors (Goldman 2012).

Eavesdropping on Discussion Groups

So what can be done about the workload for instructors that results from online discussion forums? Dividing students into groups or teams for discussion forums helps reduce the students' workload but not that of the instructor. My first advice is to realize that one ought not to feel compelled to read every post made by every student in every online forum. When an instructor has multiple small groups in a face-to-face class simultaneously discussing a topic, it is impossible for the instructor to listen to every comment made by students. Instead, instructors typically move from group to group, eavesdropping on their conversations and perhaps offering an occasional comment. The same approach can be adopted for online discussion forums. Instructors can drop in on the conversation of one or two of the groups each week by reading the posts made in a particular group. Then rotate, so over a period of weeks the instructor has dropped in on every group.

Self-Graded Participation

If participation in the online forum is a part of the course grade, the instructor has several options. One approach is to require students to assign their own grades utilizing a rubric developed by the instructor. For example, an instructor might develop a rubric similar to the following:

1 = Posted a comment or question prior to the Thursday deadline

2 = Posted a comment or question prior to the Thursday deadline and posted a response to a teammate's post prior to the Sunday deadline

3 = Posted a comment or question prior to the Thursday deadline and posted a response to a teammate's post prior to the Sunday deadline and helped to move the discussion to a deeper level through my input

4 = Posted *more than* the required comment or question prior to the Thursday deadline and posted a response to a teammate's post prior to the Sunday deadline and helped to move the discussion to a deeper level through my input

One significant advantage of this approach is that it forces students to reflect upon their own contributions to the discussion forum and how those contributions may help facilitate learning. If you are uncomfortable with students grading their own participation, students could be charged with assessing their group members' participation using a similar rubric and then the instructor could assign students the mean or the sum of the grades given by their peers.

An alternative is to require individual students on a rotating basis write a one paragraph summary of the discussion in their group's forum. The instructor would then assign discussion forum grades for all members of the group based on the summary statement. This relieves the instructor of the responsibility of reading and assessing every post to every group's forum. By utilizing one of these strategies, the instructor continues to communicate the importance of participation in discussion forums by making it a graded course activity without creating an onerous burden assessing that participation.

Changes in Forum Participation through the Semester

As we have noted, course norms are in a constant state of negotiation between instructors and students. Therefore, perhaps, it is not surprising that Cornacchione et al. (2012) found that the average number of posts per student and per discussion forum tends to decline over the course of the semester. This may be due to the novelty of the forums wearing off or less attention being dedicated to forums as a result of greater competition for students' time and energy due to other course assignments (that may comprise a more significant portion of the course grade) as the semester progresses.

Xie, Durrington, and Yen (2011), in a study of 56 students participating in discussion forums in an online course, found that students' perceptions of the value of the online discussions had a significant drop from the midpoint to the end of the semester. Students with high levels of motivation appreciated the different viewpoints expressed in forums and the opportunity to learn from and with their peers (Xie, Durrington, and Yen 2011). However, students with lower levels of motivation reported that they did not see the value of the discussion forums and felt that they did not have time to keep up with the many posts. Initially, these less motivated students participated at an equal rate with their more motivated peers, but over the course of the semester the relationship between motivation and participation in forums became stronger. The less motivated students felt forced to participate because of the impact on their grades, but expressed resentment over the requirement (Xie, Durrington, and Yen 2011). Likewise, Yao (2012) found that about one third of students enrolled in an online course did not like the required discussion forums, being unsure as to whether they contributed to learning. So while the norm in face-to-face classroom discussion may be talkers and non-talkers, online discussions may feature motivated and less motivated posters. In any case, these less motivated students do not automatically see the value of discussion forums or how they can be active co-creators of their own and their classmates' learning. It may take some explicit effort on the part of the instructor to help students understand the purpose and value of the discussion forums and to avoid creating an unreasonable workload for students.

The advice offered above applies here as well. Divide students into smaller groups for participation in online discussion forums and thereby reduce the workload for students. Requiring one-paragraph summaries of the discussion in the forum helps students see the value and importance of the forums for learning. Asking students to grade themselves forces self-reflection on one's own learning and one's contribution to the learning of others. The research also raises the question of the timing of discussion forums. It may be appropriate to have forums more frequently early in the semester when a sense of community is being developed in the course, and less frequently later in the semester as the deadlines for other course assignments draw near. Reducing the frequency of discussion forums toward the end of the semester can be a reasonable workload adjustment for both the students and the faculty member.

Increasing Participation in Online Discussions

What are some strategies instructors can utilize for increasing both the quality and the quantity of all posts in online discussions, including those made by the motivated and the less motivated students?

Make the Course Available Early

In the case of online courses utilizing discussion forums, one good piece of advice is to make the course available to students well before the course is scheduled to begin (Wagner, Garippo, and Lovaas 2011). By making the course accessible a few weeks prior to the official start date, students have the opportunity to work out technological problems and familiarize themselves with the structure of the course website as well as the format and expectations for the course itself. In addition, sending each student enrolled a personalized "welcome to the course" message with a few tips on how to navigate the course will help build a sense of social presence for the instructor and initiate the process of building community among learners. This welcome message might be part of the first discussion forum, which simply asks students to share a bit of background about themselves (major, jobs, family, pets, interest in the course, etc.) with group members in an attempt to reduce social distance among peers.

Establishing Netiquette

Just as in face-to-face courses, it is important to lay the groundwork for a safe and supportive environment if we want students to participate in discussion. Both instructors and peers play a role in fostering this supportive, collaborative community of learning (Milheim 2012). One step in this process is to clearly define netiquette expectations in the course syllabus. As we have all personally experienced, the relative anonymity provided in online forums can sometimes lead to participants interacting in ways they would not act in face-to-face settings. It is much easier to attack the person (as opposed to challenging the position) in an online forum than in a traditional classroom because one does not have to look the other in the eye and see the look of surprise or hurt in the face of the person being "attacked." Therefore, instructors need to establish guidelines for online interaction, or *netiquette*. The first rule has to be that all participants will treat all other participants with respect. While learners are encouraged to challenge one another's positions, personal attacks (e.g., "Only an idiot would see it that way" or "Only a crazy liberal could come to that conclusion") are not acceptable. Students need to learn to refute ideas and positions without attacking the person who holds the position. Another good rule of netiquette is that learners should provide evidence and logical, sound arguments to justify the positions they take. If they fail to provide such reasoning or evidence in support of their positions, they should expect that they will be asked to do so by either their peers or the instructor. It is not sufficient to say, "This is my opinion and my opinion is as good as any other opinion." In a higher education setting opinions must be supported by reason and evidence.

An instructor may want to set some netiquette rules regarding spell-checking messages prior to posting, avoiding use of all-caps (it creates the suggestion of shouting), or avoiding inappropriate personal revelations. A simple Internet search will quickly produce a variety of suggested guidelines that instructors can adapt to their courses. For example, the Indiana University School of Education Instructional Counseling program offers a good model of netiquette guidelines.[1] Once the ground rules have been laid for appropriate netiquette, instructors can turn to the task of structuring discussion forums to facilitate learning of content and the development of higher-order thinking skills.

Build Community Early in the Course

In an attempt to apply Maslow's (1943) hierarchy of needs to online courses, Milheim (2012) stressed the need to build relationships among students as well as between students and the instructor as a means of improving the quality and quantity of student posts. Creating opportunities for student-to-student interaction at the beginning of the semester is a good strategy for building community. This is a matter of importance both in hybrid courses and in courses that are offered entirely online. In a hybrid course, it's a good idea to give students some time in class to get to know their online discussion forum peers. If students have had some face-to-face interaction with their peers first, the online discussion forum is less likely to run into netiquette-related problems. Whether a hybrid or an online course, the first discussion forum

---

[1] http://www.indiana.edu/~icy/netiquette.html (June 12, 2014).

can be utilized to help students get to know their peers by structuring it as an opportunity for students to share about themselves and perhaps their motivation for enrolling in the course. By asking students, early in the semester, to share some personal information, even if trivial or unrelated to the course, it helps students to see one another as "real" people who often have plenty in common. The challenge for instructors is to create opportunities for students to feel more personally connected with each other and to be actively involved in their own learning without the instructor being at the center of the conversation (Young and Bruce 2011).

Facilitate, Don't Dominate

In online discussions, the role of the instructor is to facilitate discussion and exploration of material and ideas, not to be the authoritative voice (Shackelford and Maxwell 2012). Instructors need to participate in and guide discussion in online forums, particularly early in the semester when students will benefit from having appropriate behavior modeled for them. At the same time, instructors must carefully avoid assuming too much control of the forum, allowing, perhaps even forcing, students to take responsibility for their own and their classmates' learning and developing understanding of the course content.

Through their participation instructors can model behavior that builds a safe and welcoming community for student participation by demonstrating how to initiate discussion of a topic, acceptance of a variety of perspectives, affirmation of others' contributions, and invitations for continued input, particularly to flesh out unarticulated assumptions (Shackelford and Maxwell 2012). An instructor's timely feedback to student posts can encourage further participation, whereas a lack of instructor feedback may discourage interaction. Finding the right balance between instructor participation and making students responsible for their own and each other's learning is always a delicate balance to strike. As a general rule, the instructor likely needs to be more involved in discussion forums early in the course and less involved as the course progresses.

In order to help students understand their own role as co-creators of knowledge and understanding while avoiding the trap of the instructor taking too much control of a discussion forum, Baker (2011) argues it is important to have a clear purpose for each discussion forum that is linked to course objectives. Perhaps the most common purpose of online discussion forums is to create an opportunity for students to engage the course material interactively while also checking on comprehension. But that is not the only possible purpose. Particularly early in the course, discussion forums can serve the purpose of building a sense of community, encouraging affiliation and socialization.

Structuring Online Discussions

A well-structured discussion forum can increase student participation (Ellis 2008). However, added structure does not automatically mean students' posts will be more substantive nor that student learning will automatically increase (Ellis 2008). Just as is the case in face-to-face discussions, good questions are important, perhaps even more important in the online format. Effective discussions are based upon discussable questions, problems, debates, or situations—they should not have definitive, simple answers or be matters of unsubstantiated opinion (Mandernach et al. 2009). The type of question asked will play a significant role in whether higher-order thinking is demonstrated in an online discussion forum (Bradley et al. 2008).

Importance of a Good Question

Ertmer, Sadaf, and Ertmer (2011) examined 850 student responses in 19 online discussion forums, analyzing them in terms of Bloom's (1943) taxonomy regarding levels of thinking. They found, not surprisingly, that the questions at the higher levels of Bloom's taxonomy tended to facilitate higher levels of thinking in students' responses. In their study, brainstorming questions generated the greatest number of responses overall, while comprehension, application, and synthesis questions stimulated the most student-to-student responses (Ertmer, Sadaf, and Ertmer 2011). Lower divergent questions, which require that students synthesize and analyze information and which encourage students to consider a variety of perspectives or viewpoints, were most effective in generating high levels of student thinking in the online discussion forums.

Greenlaw and Deloach (2003), agreeing that the choice and wording of the question is likely the most critical factor in the success of online discussion forums, suggest the use of interpretive questions for facilitating critical thinking. An interpretive question can have more than one answer that can be reasonably supported from the evidence. For example, what factors contributed to the Allies' successful invasion of Normandy in World War II? Or what does the ship symbolize in *Moby Dick*? Hence students are encouraged to weigh the merits of the possible responses, contrasting and comparing, before advocating for one response or combination of responses as being better than other possibilities.

The Four-Questions Technique

Alexander et al. (2010), in a study of a graduate educational psychology course, found that a four-questions technique enhanced critical thinking in online discussions. The four-questions strategy is designed to foster *analyzing, reflecting, relating,* and *questioning* on the part of students. For example, a question at the level of analysis asks students to identify an important idea or concept in the reading. A follow-up reflection question asks students to explain why that concept or idea is important. Then students can be required to apply the concept or idea to their own experience or simply to a different context. Finally, students are encouraged to identify questions raised by the concept or idea that remain unresolved. This structured, systematic approach proved to enhance students' demonstrations of critical thinking in online forums and can be applied in a wide range of subject areas (Alexander et al. 2010).

Student-Led Discussion

Another approach, which can help instructors avoid the problem of taking too much control out of the hands of learners, is to structure discussion forums so that they are student-led or student-facilitated. Choi, Land, and Turgeon (2005) found that when thoughtfully scaffolded, student-generated questions can play a critical role in facilitating learners' reflection and knowledge reconstruction in online forums. Baran and Correia (2009) used student-led facilitation in online forums to avoid instructor dominance of discussion, to facilitate a sense of learning community, and to encourage student participation in the forums in a graduate education course. They found that student facilitators took a variety of approaches to their role. Some used a highly structured facilitation strategy that maintained close connections between the material and the discussion. Others used an "inspirational" approach, encouraging their peers to imagine ideal situations and strategies to achieve them. Still others took a practice-oriented facilitation strategy that encouraged participants to reflect on how their learning could be applied in their professional context. But regardless of the facilitation approach adopted, Baran and Correia (2009) concluded that all were able to promote meaningful exchange and high levels of participation.

However, getting students to raise the level of discussion to include higher-order thinking is not automatic or easy. In an analysis of a graduate course, Zingaro (2012) concluded that students rarely asked questions directly related to the weekly readings and did not ask questions that made connections to previously studied course material. Naranjo, Onrubia, and Segues (2012) found that high levels of participation in online forums are a necessary but not sufficient condition for high-quality contributions and concluded that the cognitive quality of online posts was generally low.

Each of these studies points to the need for careful structure and scaffolding if we want online discussion forums to be an avenue for the practice and development of students' critical thinking skills.

Christopher et al. (2004), in a study of graduate students in an education course, found no relationship between level of prompt and the thinking level demonstrated in students' responses. Higher-order prompts did not necessarily generate higher-level responses among the students in the course studied—a rather discouraging finding. Given this study was based on a single course, the results may have been skewed by the idiosyncrasies of the particular group of students enrolled in the course, the course topic, the lack of development of a sense of community in the course, or any of a number of other possibilities. Conversely and much more encouragingly, in Kearns's (2012) study of 24 online courses, asking students to relate course concepts to their own experiences did lead to a deeper level of engagement. Given the contrasting results of these two studies, one can conclude that this level of thinking, application, is likely something that instructors will need to model and provide feedback on for early attempts in order to facilitate all students' success.

O'Hanlon and Diaz (2010) discovered that high levels of student confidence are not necessarily correlated with their ability to apply concepts to real-world examples in online forums. In particular, low performers have less self-awareness than high performers and as a result tend to overestimate their abilities in this regard. Often students "don't know what they don't know." Therefore, the instructor plays an important role in improving student self-awareness and reflection as they develop higher-order thinking skills. Writing questions that cause students to be reflective, challenge them to apply new knowledge to their own experiences, or cause them to critique the evidence in support of claims can help students begin to recognize the things that they don't yet know.

It is possible that participation in online forums with both classmates and the instructor can improve demonstrations of critical thinking in other aspects of the course. In a comparison of introductory psychology courses on human development, Mandernach et al. (2009) examined critical thinking in a three-paragraph writing assignment by three course conditions: traditional face-to-face courses, interactive online courses wherein the instructor contributed to student discussion forums, and non-interactive online courses wherein the instructor did not reply to student posts in online forums. Using a critical thinking rubric to assess the writing assignment, Mandernach et al. (2009) found participants in the interactive online condition and the face-to-face condition performed similarly. However, students in the non-instructor interactive condition performed significantly lower on the critical thinking measure. This again points to the need for a careful balance between instructor control and student control in online discussion forums. The instructor's participation can facilitate the development of critical thinking skills through modeling behavior and thinking processes as long as the instructor does not inadvertently dominate discussion to the point of short-circuiting student engagement.

The same is true for student learning. Cranney et al. (2011) examined the correlations between student learning, as measured by course grade, and the number of posts in online forums. They found no correlation between the number of student posts in a given forum and learning. This result may be due to the structure of the forums. All students were required to post one comment and to respond to two other students' posts, likely leading to little variation in the number of student posts from one forum to the next in this study. However, Cranney et al. (2011) did find evidence to suggest that instructor involvement in online forums led to higher student grades. These studies support the conclusion that instructor interactivity is an important key to facilitating students' learning and development of critical thinking skills. Instructors do indeed bring added value to online discussion forums. Good teaching (instructors engaging with students) is good teaching regardless of the mode of delivery.

Conclusion

Just as with discussions in face-to-face courses, online discussion forums take forethought and careful planning in order to maximize student learning and the development of critical thinking skills. Investment of the time and energy to guide students is well-worth the effort. Whether they are an online component of a face-to-face course, a hybrid course, or a course taught entirely online, a major challenge is balancing instructor control and input in online discussion forums. Too little or too much instructor control can inhibit students' participation and learning. It will likely be the case that an instructor will need to experiment with a variety of levels of involvement and approaches over the course of several semesters to find the most appropriate balance for a given course and instructor comfort level. But excellent teachers are teachers who are willing to take some calculated risks and experiment with their courses in order to maximize student learning. So while you may not get it all right in your first effort to utilize discussion in an online format, with some planning, experimentation, and a willingness to learn from the research on the topic, online discussion can become all it's cracked up to be.

6

To Grade or Not to Grade?
And Other Conundrums

You wrapped up your grading yesterday and put another semester to bed—or so you thought. In less than 24 hours, you are getting emails, phone calls, and office visits from students who want to debate their course grades—always a frustrating situation for any faculty member. But this semester there seems to be more "grade grubbing" than usual. Much of the students' discontent centers on your decision to make participation in discussion 10 percent of the final course grade.

Admittedly, your grading of participation was very subjective. You were pretty much relying on your own impressions of who contributed how much throughout the semester. But each of these students seems to think she or he deserved a higher score than what you assigned them for participation. Maybe making something as subjective as participation a part of the course grade was not such a good idea after all.

You started off trying to keep track of students' participation by putting checks next to their names on a paper roster each time a student spoke up. That proved futile as you had trouble remembering students' names, finding them on the list, and marking checks. You were so distracted with this process that you were not listening to the students' comments and questions. Therefore, you decided to concentrate on what students were saying instead of making checkmarks and to go with your subjective impressions at the end of the semester.

But in the end that hasn't worked out so well, either. Given the number of complaints, perhaps you should have given students some feedback along the way. The quieter students in the class seem especially resentful that they did not receive full credit despite their limited participation. You wonder whether introverted students should be held to the same standard for participation as their more extroverted peers. Was it fair in the first place to require verbal participation in discussion from those extremely shy students who find it very uncomfortable? Something needs to change. These after-semester debates about grades are not something you or the students enjoy.

Grading Student Participation (or Not)

Should we make students' participation a part of their grade in the course? Responses to this question, both "yea" and "nay," are often very strongly held and defended. Some argue that because certain students are painfully shy it is unfair, unreasonable, and even unkind to require them to speak out in class. On the other hand, we require students to do many things that make them feel uncomfortable in order to either facilitate their learning or assess their learning. We require students to read difficult and challenging texts that may frustrate them. We require students to write essays and papers when they might prefer less subjective forms of assessment. We require students to take objective tests when they may prefer the opportunity to describe their learning in greater detail in a written assignment. Each of these assessment strategies will make some subset of students uncomfortable or uneasy as some prefer to write essays while others prefer objective exams. Others find reading challenging texts to be quite uncomfortable and threatening to their sense of competence and ability. Yet we require students to engage in these activities anyway because we know that they facilitate learning. If we accept the strong evidence that participation in discussion increases learning and develops critical thinking skills, why should we excuse students from this requirement when we don't excuse them from other learning activities that may make them uncomfortable? In what follows, I will attempt to explain the arguments on both sides in response to this important question regarding grading participation in discussion.

The Argument against Grading Participation in Discussion

The underlying principle against grading in general rests on an argument made by Kohn (1993) in his influential book, *Punished by Rewards*. While behaviorist approaches suggest learning can be stimulated through reinforcement with extrinsic rewards, Kohn contends that when we grade we are replacing intrinsic motivation for learning with extrinsic motivation. Instead of wanting to learn for learning's sake or out of curiosity, instead of recognizing the value inherent in new learning, students are taught to value the extrinsic reward, that is, the grade, instead. If the reward is removed, so is the desire to learn. Therefore any grading, including grading participation in discussion, can have the ironic and unintended outcome of ultimately decreasing the motivation to learn.

My friend and fellow sociologist, Diane Pike (2011), argues that point systems, in this case points for participation, cause students to focus on the wrong things (p. 4). She calls the belief that grading motivates learning a "dead idea" in teaching. Grades only motivate getting grades, not learning. Pike (2011) suggests that instead of creating complex point systems in hopes of motivating learning, instructors should focus on creating interesting and relevant assignments, provide timely feedback to students, create connections between themselves and students as well as among students, and ensure that they use class time in meaningful ways—because these are what will motivate students to learn for learning's sake (p. 6). Pike is correct. It's certainly hard to argue against investing time and energy in creating interesting and relevant assignments that motivate learning. But grading, and grading participation in particular, does not preclude one from also investing in the creation of interesting and relevant assignments. The two are not mutually exclusive.

Gilson (1994) argues that grading classroom participation, in particular, makes the classroom instructor-centered and is potentially biased in favor of males and students from western cultures. However, as noted in Chapter 3, the research on the influence of gender on participation is at best mixed and does not support the claim of bias in favor of male students. The claim of bias in favor of students from western cultures is somewhat better supported by the research—which was also noted in Chapter 3. Gilson (1994) also contends that grading participation is condescending toward students and inherently antidemocratic. However, in response to Gilson's claim, one must ask, why is grading participation any more condescending or antidemocratic than grading any other course component? Any grading system is built upon the inherent power differences between faculty and students in the classroom and functions at least in part as a control system, which can be defined as antidemocratic.

Mello (2010) provides what is perhaps the best summation of the argument against grading class participation. First, he notes that grading class participation is highly subjective and therefore dependent upon the instructor's interpretation of each student's behavior. One sure way to incite student resentment is to make participation a part of the course grade and provide no feedback to students on their participation grade until the end of the semester when, based on your general impressions, you assign a grade. In those cases it should be no surprise that students show up in your office demanding to know why they received an 85 percent on their participation grade when they think they deserved a 95 percent.

In addition, grading participation is challenging to do well (Mello 2010). How many of us have tried to keep track of student participation by keeping a roster in front us and making a checkmark each time a student speaks up? A related challenge is that you must know each student's name and be able to recall it on the spot. You must be able to quickly find the student's name on the roster. This tracking of each comment can result in losing focus on what the student is saying and of the qualitative value of the comment because we are trying to track the quantity of comments.

Third, Mello (2010) correctly surmises that some cultures, Eastern/Asian and certain Native American, do not promote active participation in learning environments and may even see it as being disrespectful to the authority of the teacher. In an articulate defense of silent students, Myers, et al., (2009) notes that many instructors fail to recognize that silent students may be quite engaged even if they are not verbally participating and that contemporary communication theory recognizes silence as one form of communicative engagement. It is always dangerous to assume that silent students are unengaged or are poor students. We have all likely had a course where the student who earned the highest grade never said a word in class the entire semester.

Finally, Mello (2010) notes that some have argued that grading participation adds no real value to class because it can lead to talking for the sake of earning a grade without contributing meaningfully to the collective learning. This final point is clearly consistent with Pike's (2011) contention that grading leads to a focus on grades, not a focus on learning. But it is inaccurate to assume that because students' participation is graded that all discussion will be "talking for the sake of earning a grade."

The Argument in Favor of Grading Participation in Discussion

At the risk of oversimplification, many of the arguments against grading participation in class discussion are arguments against grading in general. That is, after all, Kohn's (1993) thesis. One could contend that grading any student product leads to a focus on the grade instead of a focus on learning. One could argue that any grading in a course highlights the power disparities between instructor and students and is therefore inherently antidemocratic.

It is also the case that the grading of other student products, such as reflective essays, is equally subjective as grading participation in discussion—though in grading essays, the faculty member does have the time to reread and reflect upon the student's work. In grading participation, the faculty member is trying to reflect upon and assess a student's performance in real time, which is a significant disadvantage. Despite the objections, the reality is we work within a system whereby grades are the accepted measure of student achievement. They indicate, however imprecisely, a faculty member's assessment of a student's level of learning and achievement.

Grading of any type also highlights the power imbalance in the classroom as it is the instructor who is charged with assessing students' learning. We hope that the tasks that we assign and grade will encourage or require behaviors that have been shown to increase learning and will motivate learning for its intrinsic value instead of merely for the extrinsic reward of a grade. Additionally, we require students to engage in certain assessments, such as writing, not just to demonstrate their learning, but also because the act (of writing) itself facilitates learning. We give exams for which students will review and study (in hopes of earning a good grade) because we believe it will facilitate as well as measure learning. And we want students to be actively engaged in classroom discussion because it facilitates their own learning and that of their peers.

Grading is one means of providing feedback on student performance. Frequent and prompt feedback to students is one common recommendation for enhancing undergraduate education (see, for example, Braxton, Eimers, and Bayer 1996, 607). Therefore, just as instructors should provide ample and appropriate feedback on papers and other assignments, so should they provide feedback on students' participation. Grading of participation is one means through which feedback can be provided.

Mello (2010), in addition to his helpful recap of reasons not to grade participation, provides a summary of the arguments in favor of grading student participation in class discussions. First, he notes that grading participation is consistent with calls for active and engaged classrooms. As we have repeatedly noted, the one doing the most work is the one doing the most learning. An important part of the work in any classroom is verbal participation. If the instructor is the only one talking, students will not be learning as much as they could. Petress (2001) takes a particularly strong position by suggesting that when students are silent in class, they are behaving unethically because they are limiting their own learning, limiting instructor effectiveness, and failing to facilitate the learning of classmates through sharing their insights, observations, and experiences in a collaborative process of construction of knowledge and understanding. Sommer and Sommer (2007) reported that requiring and grading participation can encourage students to interact more frequently, creates a more effective learning environment, and clarifies misunderstandings. In a study that focused on how grading of participation in discussion affected undergraduate students' preparation for class, Mcdougall and Granby (1996) found that students completed more reading, recalled more information, performed better on quizzes, and felt more confident than students in a control group where participation was not required.

Second, Mello (2010) notes that grading participation often has been shown to result in better preparation and wider participation by students—not merely talking for the sake of a grade. In a survey of 258 students at a large southern university, Frisby, Weber, and Beckner (2014) reported that when participation was required students found the material to be more meaningful and perceived greater competency with that material. The authors also suggest that by requiring participation as a part of the course grade, students were likely to read more material and be better prepared to discuss the material. Somewhat ironically, while Frisby, Weber, and Beckner (2014) concluded that students learned more and liked the material more as a result of required participation, those same students reported that they were less likely to enroll in a similar course requiring participation. They conclude that while students may not enjoy participation, they are likely to learn more as a result.

Aspiranti (2011) found that there was greater and more balanced participation when students knew they were being graded or earning credit for discussion. Boniecki and Moore (2003), in a comparative study of introductory psychology classes, found students were more than twice as likely to volunteer to participate when extra-credit tokens were earned through participation. Likewise, Foster et al. (2009) found that, while not universally stimulating participation, a higher percentage of students participated in discussion when it was a part of the course grade. While students may be speaking up in class discussion in hopes of improving their grades, the act of doing so may very well also increase their learning as they are forced to be engaged and reflective in order to participate effectively.

Requiring participation prepares students for expectations they will face in the labor market (Mello 2010). Many students will someday find themselves members of work teams wherein their participation is expected. Requiring participation in college courses enables students to learn to think on their feet, which also may be necessary in a workplace environment wherein employees must interact with co-workers, supervisors, and customers.

Another reason to require participation is that it is one form of assessment that cannot be faked (Mello 2010). Students cannot plagiarize participation. They cannot copy participation by peering at another student's homework or cutting and pasting text from a website. In order to earn credit for participation, students must attend class—something that also has been linked to learning (Howard 2005)—and verbally participate to demonstrate their growing understanding.

Finally, we know that all students benefit from the active participation of peers from diverse backgrounds. By hearing and considering a variety of viewpoints and personal experiences, students' thinking and understanding are expanded (Mello 2010). Indeed, one could argue that rather than being antidemocratic, required participation in discussion is more, not less, democratic because it fosters the participation of more (if not all) class members. The contributions of students, particularly students from backgrounds distinct from the majority of classmates, can significantly enhance the learning of their peers.

Instructors grade participation in discussion in the hope of creating an inclusive learning environment with wider and more balanced participation that will result in greater learning for all class members. But how many faculty members grade participation and how do they go about creating a grading system that is fair without becoming an unreasonable burden on the instructor?

Effectively Grading Participation in Discussion

Many faculty members have at some point at least attempted to include student participation in class as a portion of their course grade. In the Frisby, Weber, and Beckner (2014) study, 69 percent of students surveyed reported being in a course that required them to participate for a grade. In a survey of over 300 faculty members in a wide range of disciplines who teach undergraduate courses of 50 or fewer students, Rogers (2011, 2013) found that 82 percent of faculty explicitly included participation as a formal expectation in the course syllabus. However, only 62 percent of instructors graded participation, with faculty in math and sciences being less likely to do so than others. Of those faculty who made participation a formal expectation, most defined participation rather broadly to include things such as class attendance as well as voluntary verbalizations. The modal percentage of the course grade attributed to discussion was 10 percent. Roughly two thirds of the faculty who graded participation collected specific data on participation other than attendance, but most indicated that they graded participation holistically without relying on specific data, suggesting faculty are not necessarily using data on participation to assign grades, even when they collect it. Based on the limited research available, we can conclude that somewhere around two thirds of faculty attempt to include participation as a part of the course grade. However, they do so in a variety of ways.

Grading Discussion on the Bubble

In a study of core curriculum syllabi at the University of Seattle, Bean and Peterson (1998) found that 93 percent of faculty included class participation as a component of the course grade. However, informal discussions with faculty members revealed that most used discussion in a rather ambiguous way when computing course grades. Instead of making participation a specific percentage of the course grade, faculty would use it as reason to raise a grade (or not to raise a grade) for students who were "on the bubble" between grade levels (e.g., from a B+ to an A–). Bean and Peterson (1998) concluded that the subjective nature and difficulty of grading participation, potential unfairness to shy students, and the difficulty of recordkeeping and defending participation grades led faculty to use discussion in this less-than-systematic manner when grading.

Awarding Points in Real Time

Others have made explicit attempts to grade participation by rewarding student comments in real time. Nelson (2010) awarded students bonus points when they participated in discussion by asking questions. He found that more than three quarters of students participated when he utilized this strategy. In a similar approach, Chylinski (2010) awarded "participation money" for quality contributions to keep track of student comments during discussion and to reinforce their participation. He even created a system wherein dominant talkers received less money for additional comments while quieter students received more money for their input. He concluded that this strategy increased the overall number of student comments during weekly class discussions, improved students' understanding of the course material, and contributed to a positive social atmosphere.

Students' Self-Grading of Discussion

Another strategy for grading discussion is to require students to reflectively grade their own participation following a rubric. For example, in seminar courses I utilize a rubric to guide students' self-assessment of their participation.

1 = Did not read the assignment and did not participate in class discussion

2 = Did not read the assignment and made one contribution to class discussion

3 = Read the assignment and made one contribution to class discussion

4 = Read the assignment and made more than one contribution to class discussion

This rubric recognizes that students may be learning something by attending class even if they did not complete the assigned reading and are not participating in discussion. It also acknowledges that students may have some knowledge of the subject matter and be able to contribute to the discussion even if they have not completed the assigned reading. But the ideal situation is that the student has prepared for class by completing the reading assignment and then contributes to class discussion in an informed and insightful way. In courses where small groups are utilized, I add an additional point to the rubric requiring that students ensure that all of their group members contribute to the conversation.

5 = Read the assignment and made more than one contribution to class discussion and made certain that every member of my group participated in discussion

This approach enlists students as my allies in ensuring that every student in the class participates. It also has the advantage of requiring the dominant talkers to restrain their own participation and invite the participation of the quieter students. No one in the group can maximize their discussion points unless everyone in the group has participated. Through their invitations to quieter students to speak up, peers help to construct a safe and welcoming atmosphere for participation.

The question that always arises when I describe student self-assessment of their participation is, "Don't students inflate their own grades with everyone always assigning themselves the maximum grade?" In my experience it is true that the majority of students assign themselves a 4 or a 5. However, it is also my experience that students are earning these grades. As I walk from small group to small group eavesdropping while students are working their way through the discussion questions I provide to guide their conversations, I hear the dominant talkers inviting the quiet students to speak up and the quiet students do so. The same is true in whole-class discussions; most students assign themselves the maximum grade but most students are also participating in an informed manner, having completed the reading assignment prior to class. Using the discussion questions in combination with this self-assessment grading rubric tends to make participants out of all students. It has the added benefit of requiring every student to reflect upon their contribution to everyone's learning, reinforcing the message that learning is a socially shared constructive process.

Research on student-graded participation affirms my personal experience. In a study of undergraduates in three sections of an educational psychology course that compared students' self-recording of their contributions to class discussion with those of observers, the researchers found a high degree of agreement between students and observers and concluded that students did not over-report their participation (Krohn et al. 2011). In another study that compared faculty evaluation, peer evaluation, and student self-evaluation of individuals' participation in discussion, students' self-evaluations were somewhat higher than faculty evaluations, but peers evaluated one another less highly than did faculty (Ryan, Marshall, Porter, and Jia 2007). However, Ryan, Marshall, Porter, and Jia's (2007) finding may have had more to do with the specific conditions of the study than being a generalizable pattern in college courses. Students were required to assign peer grades using a normalized distribution. So regardless of the amount or quality of contributions, only a small percentage of participants could receive the maximum grade.

Students are more likely to remember their own contributions than they are to be able to keep track of the contributions of a classroom full of peers, thus likely leading to a perception on the part of most students that they are participating at a rate that is greater than that of their peers. Peterson (2001) concluded that students' documentation of participation encouraged preparation to participate, participation during in-class discussions, and application of material to personal and professional situations. In sum, we should not assume that students' self-grading will lead to unjustified grade inflation. It's more likely that such an approach will result in students' consistently reflecting upon their responsibility to contribute to their own and their classmates' learning, thus causing them to contribute meaningfully more frequently.

Engaging Students in Grading Participation

Weimer in her book, *Learner Centered Teaching* (2013, 188–191), offers several self-assessment strategies that are applicable to assessing student participation in discussion. She makes the point that it is easier to look critically at one's own work after having reviewed the work of others. This strategy could be particularly helpful in an online discussion forum. The faculty member could provide students with a copy of a discussion thread that includes four or five student participants and a rubric for assessing participation. Students read the thread with the rubric criteria in mind (e.g., "Did the participant contribute new insights or simply agree with a classmate?"; "Did the participant thoughtfully respond to a peer's posting?") and assign discussion grades to each of the participants. This activity helps students understand what is expected in the way of participation and do a better job of recognizing quality participation in an online discussion forum.

Another approach (Weimer 2013) is to have students write brief reflective statements describing how their ideas have changed or their skills have developed as a result of their participation at the end of a class period. Weimer (2013) goes on to note that it is important to carefully explain to students that, rather than merely claiming they learned "so much," they need to summarize evidence that illustrates and supports their claims.

A third intriguing possibility is to assign participation partners to students (Weimer 2013). Participation partners exchange individual participation goals in writing. For a period of time, say two weeks, they observe each other's participation. At the end of the observation period, each partner provides the other with written feedback on what they have observed. Weimer (2013) notes that in her experience with this strategy, students are positive and encouraging even if their partner has not met his or her participation goals. Then at the end of the course, students write a self-assessment of their participation, justifying the grade they think they have earned. Weimer (2013) then compares these with her own assessments of students' participation based on her own notes on student participation recorded immediately following each class session. She has found that roughly 85 percent of the time she and the respective students are within three points when assigning participation grades.

Krohn et al. (2011) offer yet another approach that involves students in self-grading of their participation. Students were provided cards on which they were to record a phrase or a sentence describing their particular contribution to discussion. The first contribution was worth two points. A second contribution earned students an additional point with three points being the maximum per class period. These cards were then collected by the instructor and grades recorded. Krohn et al. (2011) found that using this method, students' self-reports correlated well with scores of observers.

In an attempt to help prepare students for assessing their own participation in class, Knight (2007) developed an intriguing strategy. Very early in the semester Knight (2007) asked students to grade their own participation on a scale that ranged from "I contribute several times during every class session" to "I rarely contribute to class discussion." Students then had to provide a brief rationale for their grade. Knight (2007) found, as she suspected, that students would assign themselves higher grades than she, the instructor, would have because they were defining participation quite broadly, including such behaviors as attendance and preparation for class. She then utilized the opportunity to provide students with feedback, helping them to understand that for the purposes of her class, participation was defined as verbal participation in class discussion.

Knight's (2007) strategy points us to this question: What are instructors assessing when they grade student participation? Indeed, some faculty members take an expansive view of participation in developing their grading rubrics (see, for example, Lathrop 2006), including students' preparation for class and engagement with and responding to peers' input. Some (for example, Chapnick 2005) even include allowing shy students to email comments and questions to the instructor after class.

But the most systematic attempt to identify what instructors are grading when they grade participation was a study by Penny and Murphy (2009). Penny and Murphy (2009) used Internet search engines to locate 50 rubrics used by college and university faculty. While they found 153 different performance criteria, they grouped them into four major categories. Almost half of all the performance criteria were categorized as *cognitive* criteria. This included assessments of critical thinking, problem solving, and use of course content in discussions. The other three criteria, each accounting for 18–20 percent of the performance criteria, were *mechanical* criteria (e.g., use of proper language, grammar, spelling, etc.), *procedural* criteria (e.g., number of comments, showing respect toward others, etc.), and *interactive* criteria (e.g., the degree to which students interacted with and responded to peers). As a faculty member develops rubrics for assessing student participation, these four criteria are helpful to keep in mind. What, precisely, is it that we want to encourage through our assessment strategies? Our answers should drive the design and development of the rubrics. If our concern is simply to get more students talking, then an emphasis on procedural criteria is appropriate. If we want to see students applying, critiquing, or analyzing course content, then a focus on cognitive criteria is most appropriate.

Should we require and grade students' verbal participation in class? As we noted in the first chapter of this book, there is good evidence that students learn more when they are engaged and participating with the subject matter, their peers, and their instructor. Grading is one means to encourage participation. Will it make some students more uncomfortable than others? Absolutely it will, but if we take steps to structure discussion in the least threatening way possible, remembering advice from earlier chapters regarding introverted students and allowing them time to reflect and collect their thoughts prior to asking them to share in front of their peers, the discomfort can be at least minimized while the learning is being enhanced.

In addition to the issue of grading student participation in discussion, there are two additional common challenges an instructor must address in order to most effectively facilitate students' learning. These are helping students recognize the learning that is happening in discussion and the issue of content coverage.

Helping Students Recognize Their Learning through Discussion

Perhaps because of our concern with ensuring that we cover all the necessary content, Fink (2003) notes that in many courses teachers are "doing an information dump" (p. xi). Such an approach allows instructors to feel as if they have lived up to their professional responsibilities by providing a rigorous, content-rich course. But is an information dump an effective approach to facilitating student learning? Trigwell's (2010) review of the scholarship concludes that when teachers take an information-transmission/teacher-focused approach, student learning tends to be at the surface level. Conversely, when the faculty member utilizes a conceptual-change/student-focused approach, students' learning tends to be much deeper (p. 33). The research in the scholarship of teaching and learning is clear; students need to do the work if they are to learn (Barkley 2010, 23). In their review of the research over a 30-year period, Pascarella and Terenzini (1991, 2005) concluded that students are likely to learn more and develop better cognitive and intellectual skills when they are interacting with their professor, their peers, and the material in a collaborative learning approach, what Weimer (2013) refers to as *learner-centered* teaching. Through a learner-centered approach, the student is the one responsible for learning.

However, doing something that is appropriate and good for students does not mean they will automatically appreciate your efforts. Sadly, it is the case that throughout their educational careers and certainly in most of their college courses, students are told the correct answers, told what they need to know, and are expected to be able to repeat those answers on an exam. In response to these conditions and experiences, students have developed strategies that allow them to play the higher education game quite successfully. They come to class, they take notes, and they memorize content long enough to repeat what they have been told on the exam. Then they move on to the next section of the course, quickly forgetting what they have memorized as they focus on a new information dump. It is a strategy that has served most college students well throughout their educational careers.

By making the decision to change the nature of the game by putting greater responsibility upon students for their own learning and discovery of answers, students will inevitably experience a sense of disruption. The old rules no longer apply and students may complain, "My professor is not telling me what I need to memorize for the exam. She is expecting me and my peers to discover what we need to know." Implied in this criticism is the recognition that simply memorizing is no longer enough to earn a good grade in the course. The change of pedagogical approach and the accompanying required changes in learning strategies is a scary prospect for students. It may feel to students that you are changing the rules of the game after the game has begun or that you are merely trying to trick them. Many students have no idea how to discern what insights have been gained through a discussion, whether it occurs in a small group, in a whole-class format, or online. What can you do as the instructor to help them develop this skill of discernment and acquire new, more effective learning strategies?

Calling Attention to Important Points Made during Discussion

We have hit upon a variety of strategies in previous chapters. But it is worthwhile to summarize them with this question in mind: How can we help students recognize what's being learned through discussion? One strategy is to structure the discussions by providing questions to students ahead of time. These discussion questions can be linked to reading reassignments. The questions provide a framework that students can use to help them grasp key points in their reading and in the subsequent class discussions. It's often a good idea to begin with a question or set of questions that ask students to recap the central argument being made by the author and the evidence that is being marshaled to support the argument. Then students can be asked to critique the argument. Is the evidence in favor of the position taken by the author convincing? What types of evidence might challenge or strengthen the author's conclusion? Is the author overlooking any important sources of evidence? Are there other compelling alternative explanations or interpretations of the evidence? If the subject is one where there is a single correct answer, questions could focus on the process rather than the outcome: "What are the steps required to solve this equation? Is this the most efficient route to solving the problem? How can we check to be certain we have found the correct answer? Can you explain the steps in the process to a classmate?"

As students move through the questions during whole-class discussion or during the recap with the entire class that follows discussion in smaller group, the instructor can use the board to highlight key points as students make them. This act signals to students that an important insight has just been offered, focuses their attention, and combats the passivity that attends students who have been conditioned through years of experience in the educational system to copy down what gets written on the board. At the same time, you can affirm the student who has made the comment and ask him or her to repeat it for emphasis: "That's a great point, Miguel! Did everyone catch what Miguel just said? He nicely summarized the author's central thesis. Miguel, would you mind repeating that so we can all be clear about it?" As Miguel repeats his point, you can write it on the board and label it "Miguel's point," which again affirms Miguel and reaffirms to the class that they can learn from one another. In addition to helping students understand the material, this approach has the added benefit of signaling to students that they are responsible for helping one another identify key insights and thereby assist with the collective construction of knowledge and understanding.

Recapping before Moving On

Another way to help students understand their role in the construction of shared meaning and understanding is to summarize the conversation related to one question prior to moving onto the next question. For example, a discussion of the gender-based wage gap might be summarized along these lines: "Okay, let's review the highlights before we move ahead. First, Chloe made an important point when she observed that while women earn less than men, women are often not working as many hours as men due to childcare responsibilities. Second, Desmond noted for us that the evidence shows that women are overrepresented in poorly paid occupations and underrepresented in more well-paid fields, which accounts in part for the wage gap. Third, Ethan countered that the author presented strong evidence to show that women earn less than men even when working in the same occupations. And, finally, Aisha raised an important critical question for us: Why do occupations dominated by women pay relatively less than occupations dominated by men? Are these occupations truly less valuable to society? Or is it perhaps because women are the majority in these occupations that the work is less well-rewarded? So with those thoughts in mind, let's move onto our second question." By connecting students by name to their contribution, you are again affirming individual students and emphasizing the collective responsibility for learning while you are summarizing the discussion in response to a particular question.

It can be challenging to keep track of the students who made particular important points, so you may need to be jotting down notes to yourself during the discussion or using the board to write down both important comments and the names of students who made the comments. Such affirmation of peers' insights can go a long way to redefining the classroom from one where the instructor is the bank of knowledge to one wherein students are active participants in the construction of knowledge and learning.

Asking the Follow-up Question

Because discussions are often rather free-flowing and represent a kind of stream-of-conscious thinking, it is important for instructors to know when and how to ask follow-up questions. As we have noted, sometimes students will skip over the rationale, evidence, and required logic supporting a conclusion, jumping straight to the conclusion itself. In those cases, it's important to ask a friendly follow-up question: "Thanks, Jeremy. I see that you think global warming is clearly occurring and is caused by human behavior. What is the evidence that convinced you this is the case?" If Jeremy stumbles and is unable to articulate his evidence, you can always ask classmates to come to his aid: "Jeremy has gotten us off to a good start by taking the position that global warming is caused by human activity. Who can cite evidence that supports this conclusion and build on what Jeremy has started for us?"

You can also ask class members to provide counterevidence when it is available. For instance, you could ask, "Someone take the role of devil's advocate and assume for a minute that you disagree with Jeremy's position on global warming. What evidence would you cite to support your position?" By asking peers to assume the role of devil's advocate you are making it safer for both them and Jeremy to disagree. Students can challenge Jeremy's position without having to say they personally disagree with Jeremy.

After the various positions on or views of a topic have been sufficiently developed, then you can ask the class to evaluate the quality and quantity of evidence for each position. You can say, "We've heard both sides of the argument. Which side has the strongest case and the best evidence to support its position?" By following this pattern of posing questions, you are requiring students to move toward higher levels of thinking. First, students must take a position. Then, they must articulate the evidence in support of the position. After that, they must present evidence that supports the counter-position. Finally, they must assess the quality of evidence and argument in determining whether one position or the other is more compelling. In so doing, we remind students that the point of discussion is not just to get people talking, but to get learners thinking and collectively expanding each other's understanding.

Encouraging Students to Prepare for Effective Discussion

A related concern, and one we have touched upon previously, is how you can ensure that students will be prepared and able to effectively contribute to discussions that are hopefully insightful and encouraging of deep learning. The answer, of course, is to design classes in such a way that students have good reason to prepare. Fink (2003) argues, "The key to getting students to do the necessary work and reading before class seems to lie in devising the right kind of in-class activities. Students need to know that the reading done beforehand will be absolutely necessary to do the in-class work *and* that the work is an important and valuable kind of work" (p. 167).

By requiring students to do the hard and messy work of learning, we motivate them to do the out-of-class work necessary to be prepared for in-class activities. By constantly reinforcing that students are expected to contribute to each other's learning and understanding, instead of relying on the instructor to tell them what they need to know, we are taking advantage of peer pressure. Students need to be prepared in order to meet their obligation to each other. We also need to design in-class activities that are interesting, engaging, and appropriately challenging (neither too easy nor too difficult) to facilitate an interest in learning for its own sake. When students find the learning inherently valuable and interesting, they are more likely to achieve at deeper levels rather than to focus on surface learning in order to pass an exam.

But I Need to Cover All This Content

A consistent fear of instructors considering adopting discussion as a pedagogical strategy is the issue of content. Many faculty members worry that if they take time away from their own lecturing to allow for discussion, they won't be able to cover all the content they wish to cover or are required to cover. On the one hand, this is a legitimate concern. Discussion is a less efficient pedagogical strategy when it comes to content coverage. It takes time for students to struggle with material and come to greater understanding and learning. It is easier and quicker just to tell them what they need to know for the test, for the next course, or for the licensure exam. However, instructors telling students something, thus merely covering the content, does not mean that students are learning.

As we have noted earlier, in their reviews of research on student learning in higher education, Pascarella and Terenzini (1991, 2005) concluded a large part of student gains in both factual knowledge (or content) and the development of cognitive skills is the result of interactions with peers and faculty both inside and outside of the classroom and that collaborative learning strategies significantly enhance learning. Fink (2003) suggests that the best thing faculty can do for students is to give them more *doing* and *observing* experiences related to the subject matter of the course (p. 123). By requiring students to articulate their growing knowledge and understanding to one another, they are doing the work in the classroom and learning in the process (Cooper, Cox, Nammouz, and Case 2008; Michael 2006). Weimer (2013) concludes that when instructors are primarily focused on covering the content, students respond by memorizing with little understanding of the subject (p. 37). Simply telling students what they need to know is not an effective way to cover the content.

This is not to say that content is unimportant. But we need to develop strategies that make students increasingly responsible for their own learning of the content and development of appropriate thinking skills. Fink (2003) contends that the learning goals set by most college faculty do not go much beyond an "understand-and-remember" type of learning (p. xi). If, as most of us claim on our syllabi, our goal is the development of critical thinking skills in students, *telling* them the content through an overemphasis on lecture will not get us there. The learner-centered approach is more challenging. It is less scripted than lecturing and requires that we as faculty think on our feet and make adjustments in real time during class sessions (Weimer 2013). But it does lead to the development of thinking skills as well as mastery of content.

Conclusion

These additional conundrums regarding grading students' participation in discussion, helping students recognize the learning that is occurring in the often free-flowing and perhaps even chaotic discussion, and determining the right balance between content and learning are challenges likely to be resolved only through trial and error. Just as mastery of any skill does not come automatically or immediately, becoming an effective facilitator of student learning through discussion will take some sustained and intentional practice. With experience will come increased facility with this pedagogical approach, and with that increased effectiveness, students will come to see how they contribute to one another's learning and be better able to assess their own contributions.

At this point students are much less likely to object to your assessments of their participation because you have been clear about your expectations and have sought to affirm students' contributions in each class meeting. Likewise, as you help students recognize the important learning that is occurring, they will understand that learning is more than memorizing what they have been told. And, finally, as you experiment with balancing deep learning with content coverage in light of your own priorities, those of your colleagues, and those of your discipline you will find that in the end student learning is more important and effective than merely telling students the content. Tackling each of these conundrums is neither easy nor automatic, but the payoff in terms of student learning and engagement makes the effort required very worthwhile.

Afterword

It has been an interesting ride this semester. On the one hand, you feel quite proud of your efforts. You listened to the faculty development specialists when they said, "The one doing the most work is the one doing the most learning." When they pointed out that in the typical college class it is the instructor, and not the students, who is doing the most work, you realized it was true in your courses. You made the commitment to have students do more of the work.

On the other hand, it's apparent that there is still room for improvement. You constantly faced the temptation to reassert your authority and expertise. Certainly, it would be more efficient in terms of the amount of content "covered" if you just told students the "right" answers instead of letting them struggle through the process of discovery. Admittedly there were even times when you missed being the star, the expert, the sage on the stage sharing the insights you have accumulated over years of teaching and research. After all, you love what you teach and you want to ignite that same passion for the subject in your students. And, frankly, you're good at it. You can be an effective performer on that stage when you need to be. But you kept reminding yourself, the one who does the work does the learning.

Admittedly, the students were mixed in their responses to your efforts. Some of them seemed to think you were abdicating your responsibility as the instructor by making them undertake the process of discovery through actively engaging with their classmates and the material in small- and large-group discussions. They have been "told" what they need to know ever since they entered the formal education system. They are accustomed to and comfortable with memorizing what they need to know—at least long enough to pass the exam. However, it's clear that once the exam is finished, most students quickly forget almost everything they have supposedly learned as they begin memorizing new material for the next exam. That is the cycle you were determined to break. Students need to learn how to learn, how to question, and how to think. You made progress toward that goal this semester.

As we have seen, 30 years of research in the scholarship of teaching and learning have demonstrated that engaged students learn more. One key strategy to engage students is through discussion. At first glance it is easy to think that discussion as a pedagogical strategy refers only to small seminar courses or to use of the Socratic method. But discussion as a pedagogical strategy can take many forms. Discussion can occur with the entire class during frequent pauses in an otherwise lecture-driven class session. Discussion can occur in small groups as students are asked to apply material or solve a problem. Discussion can occur in pairs through such classroom assessment techniques as Think-Pair-Share. Anytime one can engage students with the course content, their instructor, and their classmates, odds are good that learning will increase.

However, student engagement in discussion is not automatic. In fact, quite the opposite is true. We have seen how in the typical college classroom the norm is not that students must pay attention, but rather they must pay civil attention. In most college classrooms, creating the appearance of paying attention is generally all that is required. Therefore, instructors who wish to increase learning through engagement in discussion beginning on the first day of class must work to establish a new norm that includes engagement and participation in discussion.

Another college classroom norm that can undermine the effectiveness of discussion is the consolidation of responsibility. Without intentional efforts to change this normative expectation, roughly five to seven students will account for the vast majority of student verbal participation in class. This is true regardless of enrollment in the course. While the impact of student gender is not consistent in the research, older students are more likely to be dominant talkers, students tend to speak more frequently in courses taught by female instructors, and students from other cultures or whose native language is not English may view discussion differently than do their peers.

Students come to us with a common definition, or understanding, of the college classroom and their roles within it. They carry the baggage of years of experience in the educational system that has shaped their expectations of instructors and courses. While instructors typically see the classroom as a focused environment that requires engagement of all participants, students (particularly quieter or more introverted students) may see the classroom as an unfocused setting wherein their participation is optional. These sometimes differing definitions of the situation can lead to misunderstanding and even conflict in the classroom. Therefore it's always a good idea for instructors to have a discussion about discussion with students at the beginning of the semester, establishing the expectation for participation of all students.

As more and more students include online courses in their higher education experience, it is also important to thoughtfully consider what effective discussion looks like in an online format—be it part of an online course or an online component of a face-to-face course. Much of the same advice applies in the online context. Instructors need to provide a compelling question or problem that engages students' interest. Ground rules, or netiquette guidelines, that create a safe environment for interaction without fear of undue criticism or personal attack are necessary. Requiring students to respond to each other's posts in a thoughtful manner and modeling how to do so also helps to facilitate learning through online discussion.

Of course, successful discussions require intentional effort and structuring of the course on the part of the instructor to create opportunities and a climate that facilitates learning. One key question is whether to make participation in discussion a component of the course grade. Inevitably there will be some students who are quite uncomfortable speaking in front of their classmates. But, again, discussion need not always involve the entire class in a single conversation. Instructors can utilize small groups or even pairs to engage students in dialogue with each other. A second conundrum is how to help students recognize the learning that is happening during discussion. Often students are accustomed to instructors laying out content in a neat and orderly fashion that facilitates easy note-taking. Discussions are often much more circuitous and messy in the learning process. We need to help signal to students when important points are being made so they can begin to recognize the learning that is happening in the midst of back-and-forth dialogue. A third conundrum to consider is balancing discussion with coverage of content. Of course, the first rule to remember is that just because an instructor said something, thus covering the content, it does not mean that learning has occurred. An information dump focused on content coverage is not the most effective means to ensuring learning. An instructor has to find the appropriate balance between the amount of the content and the facilitation of learning. That balance will be influenced, not only by the instructor's personal preferences, but also by departmental, curricular, and accreditor expectations.

In many ways this book has been about how to make students do more of the work in the classroom through engaging the material via discussion with their instructor and their peers. In this process students will learn more content while at the same time developing the higher-order thinking skills we expect them to gain through higher education. But these accomplishments are not easily or hap-hazardly gained.

Left to develop and evolve in accordance with the norms oper-ative in most college classrooms, many students will choose to pay only civil attention rather than be actively engaged in classroom discussion. The discussions that do develop will be dominated by a small number of students with the majority being observers of those conversations. A large percentage of our students will con-tinue to define the classroom as a space wherein verbal participation is optional and purely voluntary. But social norms are always in a state of negotiation. Because they are social they are not etched in stone. It does not have to be this way.

We can take steps that will change the classroom norms both in our face-to-face classrooms and in online courses (or in online discussion forums associated with face-to-face classes), which will increase the percentage of students who participate. And when we thoughtfully scaffold discussions through careful planning by instructors who work to motivate students to be prepared for effective participation, an overwhelming body of research in the scholarship of teaching and learning tells us that students will learn more content and develop higher-order thinking skills.

These successes don't come easily. Just as any new skill takes practice and refinement, so does the adoption of more effective pedagogies. We don't get it all figured out the first time we try it. And we should remember that students are learning and adapting to these new strategies of engagement as well. When we are learning something new, it is normal to feel awkward and uncomfortable. Students will experience some of that same discomfort just as we as instructors will experience it, too. Students may even be openly hostile to our efforts at first. But as their experience with partici-pation in purposeful discussion grows, they will also experience the exhilaration that comes with mastering new content and refine-ment of cognitive skills. And that makes learning and teaching much more rewarding for everyone.

References

Abbad, M.M. and Albarghouthi, M. "Evaluate Students' Perceptions of the Virtual Leaning Environment at Paisley University." *International Journal of Emerging Technologies in Learning*, 2011, 6 (3), 28–34.

Allan, I. E., and Seaman, J. *Changing Course: Ten Years of Tracking Online Education in the United States*. Babson Survey Research Group and Quahog Research Group, LLC, 2013.

Alexander, M. E., Commander, N., Greenberg, D., and Ward, T. "Using the Four-Questions Technique to Enhance Critical Thinking in Online Discussions." *Journal of Online Learning and Teaching*, 2010, 6(2), 409–415.

Al-Shalchi, O. N. "The Effectiveness and Development of Online Discussions." *Journal of Online Learning and Teaching*, 2009, 5(1), 104–108.

Ambrose, S. A., Bridges, M. W., DiPietro, M., Lovett, M. C., and Norman, M. K. *How Learning Works: Seven Research-Based Principles for Smart Teaching*. San Francisco: Jossey-Bass, 2010.

Anderson, B., and Simpson, M. "Group and Class Contexts for Learning and Support Online: Learning and Affective Support Online in Small Group and Class Contexts." *The International Review of Research in Open and Distance Learning*, 2004, 5(3), 1–15.

Angelo, T. A., and Cross, K. P. *Classroom Assessment Techniques: A Handbook for College Teachers*. San Francisco: Jossey-Bass, 1993.

Ary, E. J., and Brune, C. W. "A Comparison of Student Learning Outcomes in Traditional and Online Personal Finance Courses." *Journal of Online Learning and Teaching*, 2011, 7(4), 465–474.

Ashong, C. Y., and Commander, N. E. "Ethnicity, Gender, and Perceptions of Online Learning in Higher Education." *Journal of Online Learning and Teaching*, 2012, 8(2), 98–110.

Aspiranti, K. B. "Effects of Random and Delayed Participation Credit on Participation Levels in Large College Courses." Unpublished doctoral dissertation, Department of Psychology, University of Tennessee, 2011.

Astin, A. *Achieving Educational Excellence*. San Francisco: Jossey-Bass, 1985.

Auster, C. J., and MacRone, M. "The Classroom as a Negotiated Social Setting: An Empirical Study of the Effects of Faculty Members' Behavior on Students." *Teaching Sociology*, 1994, 22(4), 289–300.

Bacabac, F. E. "From Cyberspace to Print: Re-examining the Effects of Collaborative Discussion Board Invention on First-Year Academic Writing." *Journal of Online Learning and Teaching*, 2010, 6(2), 343–352.

Bain, K. *What the Best College Teachers Do*. Cambridge, MA: Harvard University Press, 2004.

Baker, D. L. "Designing and Orchestrating Online Discussions." *Journal of Online Learning and Teaching*, 2011, 7(3), 401–411.

Baran, E., and Correia, A. "Student-led Facilitation Strategies in Online Discussions." *Distance Education*, 2009, 30(3), 339–361.

Barkley, E. F. *Student Engagement Techniques: A Handbook for College Faculty*. San Francisco: Jossey-Bass, 2010.

Barnes, C. P. "Questioning in College Classrooms." In C. L. Ellner and C. P. Barnes (eds.), *Studies of College Teaching: Experimental Results, Theoretical Interpretations, and New Perspectives*. Lexington, MA: Heath, 1983.

Bean, J. C., and Peterson, D. "Grading Classroom Participation." *New Directions for Teaching and Learning*, 1998, 74, 33–40.

Benton, T. H. "The Year of Dressing Formally." *Chronicle of Higher Education*, Jan. 25, 2008. [http://chronicle.com/article/The-Year-of-Dressing-Formally /45940/]. Retrieved June 6, 2013.

Berdine, R. 1986. "Why Some Students Fail to Participate in Class." *Marketing News*, 1986, 20(15), 23–24.

Berger, P. L., and Luckmann, T. *The Social Construction of Reality*. Garden City, NY: Anchor, 1967.

Bernard, R. M., Abrami, P. C., Lou, Y., Borokhovski, E., Wade, A., Wozney, L., Wallet, P. A., Fiset, M., and Huang, B. "How Does Distance Education Compare with Classroom Instruction? A Meta-Analysis of the Empirical Literature." *Review of Educational Research*, 2004, 74(3), 379–439.

Biggs, J. "What the Student Does: Teaching for Enhanced Learning." *Higher Education Research & Development*, 2012, 31(1), 39–55.

Bista, K. 2011. "A First-Person Explanation of Why Some International Students Are Silent in the U.S. Classroom." *Faculty Focus*, June 23, 2011.

Blanchette, J. "Questions in the Online Learning Environment." *Journal of Distance Education*, 2001, 16(2), 37–57.

Bloom, B. B. (ed.). *Taxonomy of Educational Objectives: The Classification of Educational Goals. Handbook 1: Cognitive Domain*. New York: McKay, 1956.

Bodensteiner, K. J. "Emergency Contraception and RU-486 (Mifepristone): Do Bioethical Discussions Improve Learning and Retention?" *Advances in Physiology Education*, 2012, 36, 34–41.

Boersma, P.D., Gay, D., Joens, R.A., Morrisson, L., and Remick, H. "Sex Differences in College Student-Teacher Interaction: Fact or Fantasy?" *Sex Roles*, 1981, 7(8), 775–784.

Boniecki, K. A., and Moore, S. "Breaking the Silence: Using a Token Economy to Reinforce Classroom Participation." *Teaching of Psychology*, 2003, 30(3), 224–227.

Bonwell, C. C., and Eison, J. A. *Active Learning: Creating Excitement in the Classroom*. No. 1: *ERIC Digest* 336 049. Washington, DC: ASHE-ERIC Higher Education Reports, 1991.

Bradley, M. E., Thom, L. R., Hayes, J., and Hay, C. "Ask and You Will Receive: How Question Type Influences Quantity and Quality of Online Discussions." *British Journal of Educational Technology*, 2008, 39(5), 888–900.

Braxton, J. M., Eimers, M. T., and Bayer, A. E. "The Implications of Teaching Norms for the Improvement of Undergraduate Education." *Journal of Higher Education*, 1996, 67(6), 603–625.

Brinthaupt, T. M., Fisher, L. S., Gardner, J. G., Raffo, D. M., and Woodard, J. B. "What the Best Online Teachers Should Do." *Journal of Online Learning and Teaching*, 2011, 7(4), 515–524.

Brookfield, S. D., and Preskill, S. *Discussion as a Way of Teaching: Tools and Techniques for Democratic Classrooms*. (2nd ed.) San Francisco: Jossey-Bass, 2005.

Brooks, V. "Sex Differences in Student Dominance Behavior in Female and Male Professors' Classrooms." *Sex Roles*, 1982, 8(7), 683–689.

Canada, K., and Pringle, R. "The Role of Gender in College Classroom Interactions: A Social Context Approach." *Sociology of Education*, 1995, 68(3), 161–186.

Cayanus, J. L. "Using Teacher Self-Disclosure as an Instructional Tool." *Communication Teacher*, 2004, 18(1), 6–9.

Chan, J.C.C., Hew, K. F., and Cheung, W. S. "Asynchronous Online Discussion Thread Development: Examining Growth Patterns and Peer-facilitation Techniques." *Journal of Computer Assisted Learning*, 2009, 25(5), 438–452.

Chapnick, A. "A Participation Rubric." *Teaching Professor*, 2005, 19(3), 4.

Chickering, A., and Gamson, Z. "Seven Principles of Good Practice in Undergraduate Education." *AAHE Bulletin*, 1987, 7(39), 3–7.

Choi, I., Land, S. M., and Turgeon, A. J. "Scaffolding Peer-Questioning Strategies to Facilitate Meta-Cognition during Online Small Group Discussion." *Instructional Science*, 2005, 33(5–6), 483–511.

Christopher, M. M., Thomas, J. A., and Tallent-Runnels, M. K. "Raising the Bar: Encouraging High Level Thinking in Online Discussion Forums." *Roeper Review*, 2004, 26(3), 166–171.

Chylinski, M. "Cash for Comment: Participation Money as a Mechanism for Measurement, Reward, and Formative Feedback in Active Class Participation." *Journal of Marketing Education*, 2010, 32(1), 25–38.

Clarke, S. "Peer Interaction and Engagement through Online Discussion Forums: A Cautionary Tale." *Liverpool Law Review*, 2011, 32(2), 149–163.

Clouder, L., and Deepwell, F. "Reflections on Unexpected Outcomes: Learning from Student Collaboration in an Online Discussion Forum." Paper presented at the Networked Learning Conference Proceedings, Lancaster University, UK, April 2004.

Constantinople, A., Corneilius, R., and Gray, J.M. "A Chilly Climate: Fact or Artifact?" *Journal of Higher Education*, 1988, 59(5), 527–550.

Cooper, M. M., Cox, C. T., Nammouz, M., and Case, E. "An Assessment of Collaborative Groups on Students' Problem-Solving Strategies and Abilities." *Journal of Chemical Education*, 2008, 85(6), 866–872.

Cooper, T. E. "Promoting Collaboration in Courses with Perceived Single Correct Solutions." *Journal of Online Learning and Teaching*, 2009, 5(2), 356–363.

Cornacchione, E. B., Lawanto, O., Githens, R. P., and Johnson, S. D. "The Role of Students' Professional Experience in Online Learning: Analysis of Asynchronous Participation." *Journal of Online Learning and Teaching*, 2012, 8(2), 88–97.

Cranney, M., Wallace, L., Alexander, J. L., and Alfano, L. "Instructor's Discussion Forum: Is It Worth It?" *Journal of Online Learning and Teaching*, 2011, 7(3), 337–348.

Crawford, M. and MacLeod. "Gender in the College Classroom: An Assessment of the 'Chilly Climate' for Women." *Sex Roles*, 1990, 23(3/4):101–122

Crombie, G., Pyke, S. W., Silverthorn, N., Jones, A., and Piccinin, S. "Students' Perceptions of Their Classroom Participation and Instructor as a Function of Gender and Context." *Journal of Higher Education*, 2003, 74(1), 51–76.

Crone, J. A. "Using Panel Debates to Increase Student Involvement in the Introductory Sociology Class." *Teaching Sociology*, 1997, 25(3), 214–218.

Cuthrell, K., and Lyon, A. "Instructional Strategies: What Do Online Students Prefer?" *Journal of Online Learning and Teaching*, 2007, 3(4), 357–362.

Dailey, R. "The Sound of Silence: The Value of Quiet Contemplation in the Classroom." *Faculty Focus*, April 21, 2014.

Dallimore, E. J., Hertenstein, J. H., and Platt, M. B. "Classroom Participation and Discussion Effectiveness: Student-Generated Strategies." *Communication Education*, 2004, 53(1), 103–115.

Dancer, D., and Kamvounias, P. "Student Involvement in Assessment: A Project Designed to Assess Class Participation Fairly and Reliably." *Assessment and Evaluation in Higher Education*, 2005, 30(4), 445–454.

Doyle, T. *Helping Students Learn in a Learner-Centered Environment: A Guide to Facilitating Learning in Higher Education*. Sterling, VA: Stylus, 2008.

Du, J., Durrington, V. A., and Mathews, J. G. "Online Collaborative Discussion: Myth or Valuable Learning Tool?" *Journal of Online Learning and Teaching*, 2007, 3(2), 94–104.

Ellis, H.A.H. "Discussion Structure: Does It Influence Student Participation and Learning in Online Discussions?" Unpublished doctoral dissertation, Department of Instructional Design and Development, University of South Alabama, 2008.

Ertmer, P. A., Sadaf, A., and Ertmer, D. J. "Student–Content Interactions in Online Courses: The Role of Question Prompts in Facilitating Higher-level Engagement with Course Content." *Journal of Computing in Higher Education*, 2011, 23(2–3), 157–186.

Fassinger, P. A. "Understanding Classroom Interaction: Students' and Professors' Contributions to Students' Silence." *Journal of Higher Education*, 1995, 66(1), 82–96.

Fassinger, P. A. "Professors' and Students' Perceptions of Why Students Participate in Class." *Teaching Sociology*, 1996, 24(1), 25–33.

Fassinger, P. A. "Classes Are Groups: Thinking Sociologically about Teaching." *College Teaching*, 1997, 45(1), 22–25.

Fink, L. D. *Creating Significant Learning Experiences: An Integrated Approach to Designing College Courses*. San Francisco: Jossey-Bass, 2003.

Fortney, S. D., Johnson, D. I., and Long, K. M. "The Impact of Compulsive Communications on the Self-Perceived Competence of Classroom Peers: An Investigation and Test of Instructional Strategies." *Communication Education*, 2001, 50(4), 357–373.

Foster, L. N., Krohn, K. R., McCleary, D. F., Aspiranti, K., Nalls, M. L., Quillivan, C.C., Taylor, C. M., and Williams, R. L. "Increasing Low-Responding Students' Participation in Class Discussion." *Journal of Behavioral Education*, 2009, 18(2), 173–183.

Freire, Paulo. *Pedagogy of the Oppressed: 30th Anniversary Edition*. New York: Continuum, 2006. (Originally published 1968.)

Frisby, B. N., Weber, K., and Beckner, B. N. "Requiring Participation: An Instructor Strategy to Influence Student Interest and Learning." *Communication Quarterly*, 2014, 62(3), 308–322.

Fritschner, L. M. "Inside the Undergraduate College Classroom: Faculty and Students Differ on the Meaning of Student Participation." *Journal of Higher Education*, 2000, 71(3), 342–362.

Garside, C. "Look Who's Talking: A Comparison of Lecture and Group Discussion Teaching Strategies in Developing Critical Thinking Skills." *Communication Education*, 1996, 45(3), 212–227.

Gasiewski, J.A., Eagan, M.K., Garcia, G.A., Hurtado, S., and Change, M.J. "From Gatekeeping to Engagement: A Multicontextual, Mixed Method Study of Student Academic Engagement in Introductory STEM Courses." *Research in Higher Education*, 2012, 53 (2), 229–261.

Gill, R. "Effective Strategies for Engaging Students in Large-Lecture, Nonmajors Science Courses." *Journal of College Science Teaching*, 2011, 41(2), 14–23.

Gilson, C. "Of Dinosaurs and Sacred Cows: The Grading of Classroom Participation." *Journal of Management Education*, 1994, 18(2), 227–236.

Goffman, E. *The Presentation of Self in Everyday Life*. Garden City, NY: Anchor, 1959.

Goldman, Z. "Online MBA Asynchronous Discussion Workload and Value Perceptions for Instructors and Learners: Working Toward an Integrated Educational Model for Professional Adults." *Journal of Online Learning and Teaching*, 2012, 8(3), 174–188.

Goodman, S. B., Murphy, K. B., and D'Andrea, M. L. "Discussion Dilemmas: An Analysis of Beliefs and Ideals in the Undergraduate Seminar." *International Journal of Qualitative Studies in Education*, 2012, 27(1), 1–21.

Greenlaw, S. A., and DeLoach, S. B. "Teaching Critical Thinking with Electronic Discussion." *Journal of Economic Education*, 2003, 34(1), 36–52.

Greenwood, N. A. and Howard, J.R. *First Contact: Teaching and Learning in Introductory Sociology*. Lanhan, MD: Rowman & Littlefield, 2011.

Griffiths, M. E., and Graham, C. R. "Patterns of User Activity in the Different Features of the Blackboard CMS across All Courses for an Academic Year at Brigham Young University." *Journal of Online Learning and Teaching*, 2009, 5(2), 285–292.

Hall, R. M., and Sandler, B. R. 1982. "The Classroom Climate: A Chilly One for Women?" *Project on the Status and Education of Women.* Washington, D.C.: Association of American Colleges, 1982.

Handelsman, M. M., Briggs, W. L., Sullivan, N., and Towler, A. "A Measure of College Student Course Engagement." *Journal of Educational Research,* 2005, 98(3), 184–191.

Hermann, A. D., and Foster, D. A. "Fostering Approachability and Classroom Participation during the First Day of Class: Evidence for a Reciprocal Interview Activity." *Active Learning in Higher Education* 2008, 9(2), 139–151.

Heller, J. F., Puff, C. R., and Mills, C. J. "Assessment of the Chilly College Climate for Women." *Journal of Higher Education,* 1985, 56(4), 446–461.

Heward, W. L. "Three 'Low-tech' Strategies for Increasing the Frequency of Active Student Response during Group Instruction." In R. Gardner III, D. M. Sainato, J. O. Cooper, T. E. Heron, W. L. Heward, J. Eshleman, and T. A. Grossi (eds.), *Behavior Analysis in Education: Focus on Measurably Superior Instruction.* Pacific Grove, CA: Brooks/Cole, 1994.

Hewling, A. "Culture in the Online Class: Using Message Analysis to Look Beyond Nationality-Based Frames of Reference." *Journal of Computer-Mediated Communication,* 2005, 11(1), 337–356.

Hirschy, A. S., and Wilson, M. E. 2002. "The Sociology of the Classroom and Its Influence on Student Learning." *Peabody Journal of Education,* 2002, 77(3), 85–100.

Howard, J. R. "An Examination of Student Learning in Introductory Sociology at a Commuter Campus." *Teaching Sociology,* 2005, 33(2), 195–205.

Howard, J. R., and Baird, R. "The Consolidation of Responsibility and Students' Definitions of the College Classroom." *Journal of Higher Education,* 2000, 71(6), 700–721.

Howard, J. R., and Henney, A. L. "Student Participation and Instructor Gender in the Mixed Age College Classroom." *Journal of Higher Education,* 1998, 69(4), 384–405.

Howard, J. R., James, G., and Taylor, D. R. "The Consolidation of Responsibility in the Mixed-Age College Classroom." *Teaching Sociology*, 2002, 30(2), 214–234.

Howard, J. R., Short, L. B., and Clark, S. M. "Student Participation in the Mixed Age College Classroom." *Teaching Sociology*, 1996, 24(1), 8–24.

Howard, J. R., Zoeller, A. and Pratt, Y. "Students' Race and Participation in Classroom Discussion in Introductory Sociology: A Preliminary Investigation." *Journal of the Scholarship of Teaching and Learning*, 2006, 6(1), 14–38.

Hrastinski, S. "Asynchronous and Synchronous E-learning." *Educause Quarterly*, 2008, 31(4), 51–55.

Hung, J., and Zhang, K. "Revealing Online Learning Behaviors and Activity Patterns and Making Predictions with Data Mining Techniques in Online Teaching." *Journal of Online Learning and Teaching*, 2008, 4(4), 426–437.

Jahng, N., Nielsen, W. S., and Chan, E.K.H. "Collaborative Learning in an Online Course: A Comparison of Communication Patterns in Small and Whole Group Activities." *Journal of Distance Education*, 2010, 24(2), 39–58.

Jiang, M. N. "Distance Learning in a Web Based Environment: An Analysis of Factors Influencing Students' Perceptions of Online Learning." Unpublished doctoral dissertation, State University of New York at Albany, 1998.

Johnson, D. W., Johnson, R. T., and Smith, K. A. 1991. *Cooperative Learning: Increasing College Faculty Instructional Productivity.* ASHE ERIC Higher Education Report No. 4. Washington, D.C.: George Washington University.

Junn, E. "Pearls of Wisdom: Enhancing Student Class Participation with an Innovative Exercise." *Journal of Instructional Psychology*, 1994, 21(4), 385–387.

Karp, D. A., and Yoels, W. C. "The College Classroom: Some Observations on the Meaning of Student Participation." *Sociology and Social Research*, 1976, 60(4), 421–439.

Kearns, L. R. "Student Assessment in Online Learning: Challenges and Effective Practices." *Journal of Online Teaching and Learning*, 2012, 8(3), 198–208.

Kember, D., and Gow, L. "Orientations to Teaching and Their Effect on the Quality of Student Learning." *Journal of Higher Education*, 1994, 65(1), 58–74.

Knight, D. D. *"Assessing Class Participation: One Useful Strategy." Teaching Professor*, 2007, 21 (3), 1–6.

Kohn, A. *Punished by Rewards: The Trouble with Gold Stars, Incentive Plans, A's, Praise, and Other Bribes*. Boston: Houghton Mifflin, 1993.

Krohn, K. R., Foster, L. N., McCleary, D. F., Aspiranti, L. B., Nalls, M. L., Quillivan, C. C., Taylor, C. M., and Williams, R. L. "Reliability of Students' Self-Recorded Participation in Class Discussion." *Teaching of Psychology*, 2011, 38(1), 43–45.

Kuh, G. D., Kinzie, J., Schuh, J. H., Whitt, E. J., and Associates. *Student Success in College: Creating Conditions That Matter*. San Francisco: Jossey-Bass, 2005.

Lannutti, P. J., and Strauman, E. C. "Classroom Communication: The Influence of Instructor Self-disclosure on Student Evaluations." *Communication Quarterly*, 2006, 54(1), 89–99.

Lathrop, A. H. "Teaching How to Question: Participation Rubrics." *Teaching Professor*, 2006, 20(3), 4–5.

Leonard, D. "My Life in the Classroom, Where Race Always Matters." *Vitae*. [https://chroniclevitae.com/news/504-my-life-in-the-classroom-where-race-always-matters?cid=at&utm_source=at&utm_medium=en]. May 20, 2014.

Lewis, M., and Hanc, J. "Encouraging Students to Be Readers: Survey Results of Successful Practices." *Teaching Journalism and Mass Communication*, 2012, 2(1), 12–20.

Loftin, C., Davis, L. A., and Hartin, V. "Classroom Participation: A Student Perspective." *Teaching and Learning in Nursing*, 2010, 5(3), 119–124.

Mandernach, B. J., Forrest, K. D., Babutzke, J. L., and Manker, L. R. "The Role of Instructor Interactivity in Promoting Critical Thinking in Online and Face-to-Face Classrooms." *Journal of Online Learning and Teaching*, 2009, 5(1), 49–62.

Maslow, A. H. "Theory of Motivation." *Psychological Review*, 1943, 50(4), 370–396.

Mcdougall, D., and Granby, C. "How Expectation of Questioning Method Affects Undergraduates' Preparation for Class." *Journal of Experimental Education*, 1996, 65(1), 43–54.

McHugh, P. *Defining the Situation: The Organization of Meaning in Social Interaction*. Indianapolis: Bobbs-Merrill, 1968.

McKeachie, W. J. "Research on College Teaching: The Historical Background." *Journal of Educational Psychology*, 1990, 82(2), 189–200.

Mello, J. A. "The Good, the Bad and the Controversial: The Practicalities and Pitfalls of the Grading of Class Participation." *Academy of Educational Leadership Journal*, 2010, 14(1), 77–97.

Meyer, K. A. "Evaluating Online Discussions: Four Different Frames of Analysis." *Journal of Asynchronous Learning Networks*, 2004, 8(2), 101–114.

Michael, J. "Where's the Evidence that Active Learning Works?" *Advances in Physiological Education*, 2006, 30(4), 159–167.

Milheim, K. L. "Toward a Better Experience: Examining Student Needs in the Online Classroom through Maslow's Hierarchy of Needs Model." *Journal of Online Learning and Teaching*, 2012, 8(2), 159–171.

Murray, H. G., and Lang, M. 1997. "Does Classroom Participation Improve Student Learning?" *Teaching and Learning in Higher Education*, 1997, 20, 7–9.

Mustapha, S. M. "Understanding Classroom Interaction: A Case Study of International Students' Classroom Participation at One of the Colleges in Malaysia." *International Journal for the Advancement of Science and the Arts*, 2010, 1(2), 91–99.

Myers, S. A. "The Relationship between Perceived Instructor Credibility and College Student In-Class and Out-of-Class Communication." *Communication Reports*, 2004, 17(2), 129–137.

Myers, S. A., and Claus, C. J. "The Relationship between Students' Motives to Communicate with Their Instructors and Classroom Environment." *Communication Quarterly*, 2012, 60(3), 386–402.

Myers, S. A., Horan, S. M., Kennedy-Lightsey, C. D., Madlock, P. E., Sidelinger, R. J., Byrnes, K., Frisby, B., and Mansson, D. H. "The Relationship between College Students' Self-Reports of Class Participation and Perceived Instructor Impressions." *Communication Research Reports*, 2009, 26(2), 123–133.

Myers, S. A., and Rocca, K. A. 2001. "Perceived Instructor Argumentativeness and Verbal Aggressiveness in the College Classroom: Effects on Student Perceptions of Climate, Apprehension, and State Motivation." *Western Journal of Communication*, 2001, 65(2), 113–137.

Nakane, I. "Negotiating Silence and Speech in the Classroom." *Multilingua*, 2005, 24(1), 75–100.

Naranjo, M., Onrubia, J., and Segues, M. T. "Participation and Cognitive Quality Profiles in an Online Discussion Forum." *British Journal of Educational Technology*, 2012, 43(2), 282–294.

Nelson, K. G. "Exploration of Classroom Participation in the Presence of a Token Economy." *Journal of Instructional Psychology*, 2010, 37(1), 49–56.

Nunn, C. E. "Discussion in the College Classroom: Triangulating Observational and Survey Results." *Journal of Higher Education*, 1996, 67(3), 243–266.

Ogbu, J.U. and Wilson, J., Jr. *Mentoring Minority Youth: A Framework*. New York: Institute for Urban and Minority Education, 1990.

O'Hanlon, N., and Diaz, K. R. "Techniques for Enhancing Reflection and Learning in an Online Course." *Journal of Online Learning and Teaching*, 2010, 6(1), 43–54.

O'Neal, K. "The Comparison between Asynchronous Online Discussion and Traditional Classroom Discussion in an Undergraduate Education Course." *Journal of Online Learning and Teaching*, 2009, 5(1), 88–96.

Packard, J. "The Impact of Racial Diversity in the Classroom: Activating the Sociological Imagination." *Teaching Sociology*, 2011, 41(2), 144–158.

Pascarella, E. T., and Terenzini, P. T. *How College Affects Students: Findings and Insights from Twenty Years of Research*. San Francisco: Jossey-Bass, 1991.

Pascarella, E. T., and Terenzini, P. T. *How College Affects Students: A Third Decade of Research*. San Francisco: Jossey-Bass, 2005.

Pearson, J. C., and West, R. "An Initial Investigation of the Effects of Gender on Student Questions in the Classroom: Developing a Descriptive Base." *Communication Education*, 1991, 40(1), 22–32.

Penny, L. and Murphy, E. 2009. "Rubrics for Designing and Evaluating Online Asynchronous Discussions." *British Journal of Educational Technology*, 40(5), 804–820.

Peters, K. A. "Creative Use of Threaded Discussion Areas." [http://www.cordonline.net/mntutorial2/module_2/Reading%202-2%20using%20discussion%20areas.pdf] Dec. 2013.

Peterson, R. M., "Course Participation: An Active Learning Approach Employing Student Documentation." *Journal of Marketing Education*, 2001, 23(3), 187–19 4.

Petress, K. "The Ethics of Student Classroom Silence." *Journal of Instructional Psychology*, 2001, 28 (2), 104–107.

Pike, D. L. "The Tyranny of Dead Ideas in Teaching and Learning." *Sociological Quarterly*, 2011, 52(1), 1–12.

Pitt, R. N., and Packard, J. "Activating Diversity: The Impact of Student Race on Contributions to Course Discussions." *Sociological Quarterly*, 2012, 53(2), 295–320.

Pogue, L. L., and AhYun, K. "The Effect of Teacher Nonverbal Immediacy and Credibility on Student Motivation and Affective Learning." *Communication Education*, 2006, 55(3), 331–344.

Prince, M. J. "Does Active Learning Work? A Review of the Research." *Journal of Engineering Education*, 2004, 93(3), 223–231.

Reason, R. D., Terenzini, P. T., and Domingo, R. J. "First Things First: Developing Academic Competence in the First Year of College." *Research in Higher Education*, 2006, 47(2), 149–175.

Reda, M. M. *Between Speaking and Silence: A Study of Quiet Students*. Albany, NY: SUNY, 2009.

Redmond, D. L. "A Black Female Professor Struggles with 'Going Mean.'" *Chronicle of Higher Education*. [http://chronicle.com/article/A-Black-Female-Professor/146739/]. May 27, 2014.

Roberts, K. A. "Ironies of Effective Teaching: Deep Structure Learning and Constructions of the Classroom." *Teaching Sociology*, 2002, 30(1), 1–15.

Rogers, S. L. "Grading Participation in College Courses: Instructor Attitudes and Practices." Unpublished doctoral dissertation, University at Albany, State University of New York, 2011.

Rogers, S. L. "Calling the Question: Do College Instructors Actually Grade Participation?" *College Teaching*, 2013, 61(1), 11–22.

Rourke, L., and Kanuka, H. "Learning in Communities of Inquiry: A Review of the Literature." *Journal of Distance Education*, 2009, 23(1), 19–48.

Ruan, J., and Griffith, P. L. "Supporting Teacher Reflection through Online Discussion." *Knowledge Management & E-Learning: An International Journal*, 2011, 3(4), 548–561.

Ruane, J. M., and Cerulo, K. A. *Second Thoughts: Seeing Conventional Wisdom through the Sociological Eye, Fourth Edition*. Thousand Oaks, CA: Pine Forge Press, 2008.

Ryabov, I. "The Effect of Time Online in Grades in Online Sociology Courses." *Journal of Online Learning and Teaching*, 2012, 8(1), 13–23.

Ryan, G. J., Marshall, L. L., Porter, K., and Jia, H. 2007. "Peer, Professor and Self-evaluation of Class Participation." *Active Learning in Higher Education*, 2007, 8(1), 49–61.

Sagayadevan, V., and Jeyaraj, S. "The Role of Emotional Engagement in Lecturer-Student Interaction and the Impact on Academic Outcomes of Student Achievement and Learning." *Journal of the Scholarship of Teaching and Learning*, 2012, 12(3), 1–30.

Schrire, S. "Knowledge Building in Asynchronous Discussion Groups: Going Beyond Quantitative Analysis." *Computers & Education*, 2006, 46(1), 49–70.

Semenza, G. "Professing Through the Years." *Vitae*. [https://chroniclevitae.com/news/480-professing-through-the-years]. May 6, 2014.

Shachar, M., and Neumann, Y. "Twenty Years of Research on the Academic Performance Differences between Traditional and Distance Learning: Summative Meta-Analysis and Trend Examination." *Journal of Online Learning and Teaching*, 2010, 6(2), 318–334.

Shackelford, J. L., and Maxwell, M. "Contribution of Learner-Instructor Interaction to Sense of Community in Graduate Online Education." *Journal of Online Learning and Teaching*, 2012, 8(4), 248–260.

Sher, A. 2008. "Assessing and Comparing Interaction Dynamics, Student Learning, and Satisfaction within Web-based Online Learning Programs." *Journal of Online Teaching and Learning*, 2008, 4(4), 446–458.

Sidelinger, R. J. "College Student Involvement: An Examination of Student Characteristics and Perceived Instructor Communication Behaviors in the Classroom." *Communication Studies*, 2010, 61(1), 87–103.

Sidelinger, R. J., and Booth-Butterfield, M. "Co-constructing Student Involvement: An Examination of Teacher Confirmation and Student-to-Student Connectedness in the College Classroom." *Communication Education*, 2010, 59(2), 165–184.

Sixsmith, A., Dyson, L. E., and Nataatmadja, I. "Improving Class Participation in IT Tutorials and Small Lectures." Paper presented at the 17th Australasian Conference on Information Systems, Adelaide, Dec. 2006.

Smith, D. G. 1977. "College Classroom Interactions and Critical Thinking." *Journal of Educational Psychology*, 1977, 69(2), 180–190.

Smith, M.K., Wood, W.B., Adams, W.K., Wieman, C., Knight, J.K., and Su, T.T. "Why Peer Discussion Improves Student Performance on In-Class Concept Questions." *Science*, 2009, 323, 122–124.

Sommer, R., and Sommer, B. A. "Credit for Comments, Comments for Credit." *Teaching of Psychology*, 2007, 34(2), 104–106.

Stein, G. *Tender Buttons*. Mineola, NY: Dover, 1997. (Originally published 1914.)

Stewart, C., Bachman, C., and Babb, S. "Replacing Professor Monologues with Online Dialogues: A Constructivist Approach to Online Course Template Design." *Journal of Online Learning and Teaching*, 2009, 5(3), 511–521.

Svinicki, M. D. *Learning and Motivation in the Postsecondary Classroom*. Bolton: Anker, 2004.

Svinicki, M. "Flipped Classrooms: Old or New?" *National Teaching and Learning Forum*, 2013, 22(5), 12.

Talbert, Robert. "Flipped Learning Skepticism: Can Students Really Learn on Their Own?" *Casting Out Nines*. [http://chronicle.com/blognetwork /castingoutnines/2014/04/30/flipped-learning-skepticism-can-students-really-learn-on-their-own/]. April 30, 2014a.

Talbert, Robert. "Flipped Learning Skepticism: Do Students Want to Have Lectures?" *Casting Out Nines*. [http://chronicle.com/blognetwork/castingoutnines /2014/05/05/flipped-learning-skepticism-do-students-want-to-have-lectures/]. May 5, 2014b.

Tannen, D. *You Just Don't Understand: Men and Women in Conversation*. New York: Ballantine, 1991.

Tanner, K. D. "Talking to Learn: Why Biology Students Should Be Talking in Classrooms and How to Make It Happen." *CBE—Life Sciences Education*, 2009, 8(2), 89–94.

Tatar, S. "Classroom Participation by International Students: The Case of Turkish Graduate Students." *Journal of Studies in International Education*, 2005, 9(4), 337–355.

Trigwell, K. "Teaching and Learning: A Relational View." In J. C. Hughes and J. Mighty (eds.), *Taking Stock: Research on Teaching and Learning in Higher Education*. Montreal: McGill-Queen's University Press, 2010.

Trosset, C. "Obstacles to Open Discussion and Critical Thinking: The Grinnell College." *Change*, 1998, 30(5), 44–49.

Trujillo, C. M. "A Comparative Examination of Classroom Interactions between Professors and Minority and Non-Minority College Students." *American Educational Research Journal*, 1986, 23(4), 629–642.

Umbach, P. D., and Wawrzynski, M. R. "Faculty Do Matter: The Role of College Faculty in Student Learning and Engagement." *Research in Higher Education*, 2005, 46(2), 153–184.

Wagner, S. C., Garippo, S. L., and Lovaas, P. "A Longitudinal Comparison of Online versus Traditional Instruction." *Journal of Online Learning and Teaching*, 2011, 7(1), 68–73.

Weaver, R. R., and Qi, J. "Classroom Organization and Participation: College Students' Perceptions." *Journal of Higher Education*, 2005, 76(5), 570–601.

Weimer, M. *Learner-Centered Teaching: Five Key Changes to Practice, Second Edition*. San Francisco: Jossey-Bass, 2013.

Weimer, M. "Class Discussion Challenge: Getting Students to Listen and Respond to Each Other's Comments." *Faculty Focus*, April 23, 2014.

White, J. W. "Resistance to Classroom Participation: Minority Students, Academic Discourse, Cultural Conflicts, and Issues of Representation in Whole Class Discussions." *Journal of Language, Identity & Education*, 2011, 10(4), 250–265.

Wolff, B. G., and Dosdall, M. R. "Weighing the Risks of Excessive Participation in Asynchronous Online Discussions against the Benefits of Robust Participation." *Journal of Online Learning and Teaching*, 2010, 6(1), 55–61.

Xie, K., Durrington, V., and Yen, L. L. "Relationship between Students' Motivation and their Participation in Asynchronous Online Discussions." *Journal of Online Learning and Teaching*, 2011, 7(1), 17–29.

Yao, Y. "Student Perceptions of Hybrid Discussion Format." *Journal of Online Learning and Teaching*, 2012, 8(4), 288–297.

Young, S., and Bruce, M. A. "Classroom Community and Student Engagement in Online Courses." *Journal of Online Learning and Teaching*, 2011, 7(2), 219–230.

Zingaro, D. "Student Moderators in Asynchronous Online Discussion: A Question of Questions." *Journal of Online Learning and Teaching*, 2012, 8(3), 159–173.

Index

free